INTERNAL INVESTIGATION

A Journey into Your Soul

Marvin Scott

Scripture quotations noted KJV are taken from the HOLY BIBE: King James Version

Scripture quotations noted AMPC are taken from the HOLY BIBLE: Amplified Bible, Classic Edition Copyright © 1954, 1958, 1962, 1964, 1965, 1987 by The Lockman Foundation

Scripture quotations noted ISV are taken from the HOLY BIBLE: International Standard Version Copyright © 1995-2014 by ISV Foundation. All rights reserved internationally.

Scripture quotations noted AMP are taken from the HOLY BIBLE: Amplified Bible Copyright © 2015 by The Lockman Foundation, La Habra, CA 90631. All rights reserved.

Scripture quotations noted NIV are taken from the HOLY BIBLE: New International Version®, NIV® Copyright ©1973, 1978, 1984, 2011 by Biblica, Inc.®

Scripture quotations noted NLT are taken from the HOLY BIBLE: New Living Translation, copyright © 1996, 2004, 2015 by Tyndale House Foundation. Used by permission of Tyndale House Publishers, Inc., Carol Stream, Illinois 60188. All rights reserved.

ISBN-13: 978-0-9760231-1-1

Book and Cover design by Dr. Lydia Murphy (drmartz@gmail.com)

CONTENTS

Preface iv

INTERNAL INVESTIGATION 1

DO YOU PROMISE TO KNOW THE WHOLE TRUTH? 15

BEWARE OF PROGRESSIVE TRUTH 31

THE THREE-PART BEING...52

THE SPIRIT OF MAN... 89

THE SOUL OF MAN 101

THE MATRIX OF THE MIND 121

THE LAW OF REQUISITE VARIETY 130

CHANGING THE WAY WE THINK....................................137

ZOOMED IN AND FOCUSED 150

NOT MY WILL BUT THY WILL BE DONE 156

THE HELMET OF SALVATION 172

GUARD YOUR EMOTIONS...179

WHAT DO YOU VALUE?...191

TRANSCEND..197

THE ILLUSION OF CHOICE..207

CONCLUSION 219

PREFACE

Have you ever gotten tired of being sick and tired? I don't know about you, but I found myself in a place where I wanted something different for my life. I could not tell you what I wanted, but I knew where I was in life and what I was doing was not fulfilling me. It was crazy. I wanted something different, but I kept doing the same things over and over. Have you ever been in a situation where you felt bad about what you were doing or how you were living, and yet you kept doing the same things? On the outside, I presented one way, but on the inside, I was in turmoil. I desired to live a more purposeful life, but I didn't know where to start. I can remember riding in my car one day with tears in my eyes. It was at that moment that I began to cry out to GOD asking him why and asking for His help. At that time, I did not feel as though he heard me or let alone answered me, but as I look back over my life, I realized that He did. He took me on a journey into my soul. I understand better now that this journey was actually an investigation. I began with the outside, examining my results and following a trail that eventually led back to my inner man.

It is my sincerest prayer as you read this book, the Spirit of the living GOD will speak to you as it did me, and it will lead you down the path of self-discovery. I pray that you experience His presence and power. This book is not intended to be a quick read, but rather a guide designed to provoke deep thought and self-reflection. It will challenge you by asking questions that will force you to examine your actions as well as your inner man. Therefore, a notebook is highly recommended to fully experience all this book has to offer. Enjoy, as the journey to your self-discovery begins.

INTERNAL INVESTIGATION

The book of Psalms chapter thirty-seven verse four tells us to delight ourselves in the LORD, and He will give us the desires of our heart. In the above passage, the Hebrew word that is transliterated as delight occurs approximately ten times in the bible. It comes from a primitive Hebrew root that literally means to be soft or pliable as well as delight. Often times we are quick to interpret the Psalms thirty-seven verse four as if it is telling us to take great pleasure in the LORD; however, if we look again we could possibly say the passage like this: Make yourself soft or pliable in the hands of the LORD, and He will give or put desires in your heart. Commit or roll the course of your life unto the Him and trust also in the LORD; and He will bring them all to pass (Psalms 37:4-5). When we look at it in this manner, we begin to see that some of our desires are internal, but they are not intrinsic. They are growing inside of us, but they did not start with us nor did they initially belong to us. I heard it said that if a desire comes from GOD, it has been placed there by Him as proof that you can have it. All you have to do is commit to Him and go after it. I can remember when I began to have a strong desire to fulfill GOD's purpose for my life. When I think about it, it seems to have come out of nowhere. I mean one day I am doing my own thing without a thought of GOD or his plan, and the next day I found myself praying "LORD whatever your will is for my life don't let me miss it." This became a daily prayer (multiple times a day). Was this desire intrinsic or was it just internal? This is important to understand that some things may be internal (inside our mind), but they are not necessarily intrinsic to who we are. Intrinsic is defined as belonging to the essential nature or constitution of a thing. It belongs to a thing by its very nature. While the word "internal" is defined as existing within the limits or surface of something. Internal is also defined as something that is coming from, produced or motivated by the psyche or inner recesses of the mind. Very simply put, internal tells us where something is located, where it is occurring or where it comes from; whereas, intrinsic tells us where it belongs based on its nature and composition. Every thought that occurs in our mind is internal; however, not all of our thoughts are intrinsic. Some of our thoughts are seeds or suggestions that have been sown by someone else. They are in our mind, but they were not fundamentally a part of who we are. Did Eve have an intrinsic wish to disobey GOD and eat from the forbidden tree or was the desire placed in her head by the serpent during their conversation? Was man's first sin intrinsic to his nature or was a seed sown into his mind? It is the power of suggestion. We see this at work with Moses and Jethro, his father-in-law. Moses did not complain to GOD about having to sit down and judge the people from morning until evening; until his father-in-law questioned by saying, "Why do you alone sit as judge?" After Jethro said, "What you are doing is not good. You will surely wear yourself out because the task is too heavy for you. You cannot do this by yourself." All of a sudden, we find Moses complaining to GOD. Moses is feeling like GOD does not favor him. Moses asked the LORD "Why did you bring all this trouble to your servant?" In verse fourteen of the book of Numbers the eleventh chapter Moses says to the LORD "I cannot carry this whole nation alone. The burden of this is too heavy for me." Moses finishes his conversation by asking the LORD to kill him, if he had to continue being responsible for doing all of this by himself (Exodus 18: 13-27 and Numbers 11:10-16). I am not saying that what Jethro said was wrong; nevertheless, I am asking, "would Moses have felt the same way if he did not hear his father-in-law say it first?" If you look closely at Exodus the eighteen chapter and the eighteenth verse and compare it with Numbers the eleventh chapter verse fourteen, we will find that Moses is now saying the same thing that Jethro said. At first, Moses appeared to look at the duty of judging all of the people as an honor; but, after his conversation with Jethro, he now sees the same task as a burden. Question, has that ever happened to you? Have you ever found yourself struggling to continue to believe and go after the desires of your heart because of the doubt that came out of someone else's mouth? We must not lose sight of the fact, that the Word of GOD declares that in the multitude of counsel, there is safety (Proverbs 11:14). We must learn to discern between godly wisdom, worldly counsel, and doubt. We cannot get so emotional that we fail to distinguish good advice from someone who is speaking or sowing fear into our heart. When we look at the big picture, we must determine where our thoughts, fears, and ideas are coming from. This is an internal affair. We can only find the answers by looking within.

Matthew 13:24-30 (KJV)
Another parable put he forth unto them, saying, The kingdom of heaven is likened unto a man which sowed good seed in his field: Vs25 But while men slept, his enemy came and sowed tares among the wheat, and went his way. Vs26 But when the blade was sprung up and brought forth fruit, then appeared the tares also. Vs27 So the servants of the householder came and said unto him, Sir, didst not thou sow good seed in thy field? From whence then hath it tares? Vs28 He said unto them, An enemy hath done this. The servants said unto him, Wilt thou then that we go and gather them up? Vs29 But he said, Nay; lest while ye gather up the tares, ye root up also the wheat with them. Vs30 Let both grow together until the harvest: and in the time of harvest, I will say to the reapers, Gather ye together first the tares, and bind them in bundles to burn them: but gather the wheat into my barn.

In the same way that the LORD wants to sow the Word of GOD into our heart and mind; Satan wants to sow seeds of disbelief and fear. The serpent asked the woman "Did GOD really say, 'You cannot eat from every tree that is in the garden'?" You see sin did not become intrinsic to the nature of man until after Adam's initial disobedience or after Satan's suggestion. It was after the devil's counsel to the woman and man's disobedience that Adam began to have children in his image and after his likeness. As a result, the wickedness of man became great in the earth, and the very imagination and intention of human thinking were evil continually (Genesis 6:5). The Bible declares that iniquity was found in Satan

(Ezekiel 28:15), and we must realize that he, in turn, sowed a seed of iniquity in the mind of the woman. The soul of man was corrupted by the tainted seed of the devil. As a mortal being, we have gone from a place where GOD sees us like Him, to a place where He sees our heart as deceitful more than anything else. GOD sees our heart (the feelings, the will and the intellect) as something that is exceedingly perverse and immoral. The Bible declares that the heart, carnal nature, and mind, of man, is mortally ill (Jeremiah 17:9). The Word of GOD declares that in our carnal condition, the heart of man is so sick and perverse that we cannot perceive nor understand what is in our own heart and mind. The Bible admonishes us to cast down imaginations (reasoning, and ways of thinking) and every high thing that exalts itself against the knowledge of GOD.

This book is titled "Internal Investigation" because we all must investigate our daily acts and deed to determining if the thought or source of these actions are intrinsic to our nature or were they sown by the power of suggestions. The Office of Internal Affairs is described as a unit or department within an agency (i.e., law enforcement) that investigates incidents or suspicions of criminal behavior and misconduct committed by individuals/members within that agency. One of the main goals of the Office of Internal Affairs is to ensure that illegal activities that may be occurring within an organization are not systemic or intrinsic to its normal everyday function. An example of this is discrimination and acts of violence due to racism. An individual in their mind may not discriminate;

however, working within a flawed system may cause them to unconsciously perform discriminatory actions. Many of us will say drug addiction is an addiction regardless of the drug. Nevertheless, our system categorizes, labeling crack cocaine users as criminals while those that are addicted to prescription drugs are now tagged as sick and in need of help. Users of powdered cocaine received lighter sentencing than individuals using crack cocaine. You see the same officer could have arrested both; however, the system discriminated giving users of the identical basic substance different punishments. If a white male walks into a bank or a school and shoots a group of people and is arrested alive while a black man selling CDs is killed by the police? Question, is the problem with the system or the individual. Some would say that it is based on the individual case or scenario. This could be true but what if we can go through case after case seeing this same trend? What if the system that is designed to arrest and punish the individual officers who commit such crimes fails to do its job? Is the problem intrinsic to the system or is it just internal? I want to make sure we understand I believe that there are more good police officers than bad; however, the overall system allows the bad to get away with things, and that should not be. It takes a special person to become a police officer, become a fireman, or serve in the armed forces. However, several individuals put on the uniform and perpetrate as a first responder, but malice is in their hearts.

One major systemic problem is that we come to the rescue of one of our own, even if they are completely wrong and should be punished to the full extent of the law. If we take an honest look on the inside, we will see that what I am saying is correct. This is true with most groups, organizations, families, and even churches. How many uncles, priest, or preachers have gotten away with molesting children because we did not want to punish one of our own? I cannot speak for everyone, but I am sure that many blacks were excited that OJ was found not guilty. Not because they thought, he was innocent, but rather they were happy because the system worked in a black person favor for once, and they ran to the rescue of one of their own. How many cases before and after the Rodney King incident has occurred where white men were not convicted of an obvious crime they committed. You have a group of officers standing around beating Rodney King while he is on the ground, caught on video. How many good and moral law enforcement officers saw this, and yet they said nothing? They are going against how they actually felt, running to the rescue of their own and defending their actions. The jury sees the video and still says not guilty. In a system that is functioning appropriately, this should never be. I wonder if Black America would have responded differently if the verdict was guilty. I wonder if we would have to say that black lives matter if the system treated them as if they did. All lives do matter, and if the system demonstrated this belief, there would not be a need to distinguish based on racial classification. I said system because overall first responders deserve our support, but the system allows cancers to remain unchecked and unresolved. In the book of Acts the sixth chapter, we find a group of Grecians having to say to that Greek widow's matter. The system was designed such that all widows should receive a daily distribution of food regardless of their ethnicity; however, a complaint had to be made because internally the system was not working. After an internal audit, the Apostles created a position in the church to ensure that no widow would be neglected again. Now, if the system has been adjusted fixing a problem, and the problem is still occurring, it is no longer the system but the individuals responsible for the everyday workings of it. In the same way that the temple can be used as a metaphor for the spirit, soul, and body of man; everything that has been said concerning America, law enforcement, etc. is a metaphor for what goes on inside of us day after day. How many times have we done something that adversely affected someone else, and we came up with an excuse trying to justify our actions? Why do we do this when we know that we were wrong? Thus, we are running to our own defense. When we do that it goes against our internal moral compass creating a sense of conviction or condemnation. These feelings have an adverse effect on our emotional state, which results in inner turmoil. As a result of this inner turmoil, we try to justify, our actions thus explaining why we should not feel bad, or we attempt to create a new parameter for which we consider moral, just, and true. Has the system that America was founded upon shifted its moral compass or is it the people within the system pushing for a change? America was founded as one nation UNDER GOD indivisible with liberty and justice for all; however, as a nation, we continue to push further and further away from GOD. Why is this happening? Often times because we have difficulty conforming to or measuring up to GOD's moral plumb line. A plumb line, also known as a plummet, is a cord with a weight attached to one end. The cord is held in a way to allow the weight to hang freely. This is done to determine the exact vertical. A plumb line is an objective measuring tool used to determine a true vertical or perpendicular line.

The plumb line is considered the standard, by which straightness is measured, and it does not change or move with the whims of the man, neither does the Word of GOD. It remains true, and all of our work or actions must line up with it or risk being crooked. We must continue to conduct internal audits to ensure that our affairs are in alignment with GOD's standard, and at the same time, we must consistently make inward adjustments to ensure that we are staying on the straight and narrow path. The LORD declared to the prophet Isaiah that He would make justice (right decision) the measuring-line, and righteousness the weight (plummet). Moreover, the LORD stated to the prophet Amos that he was setting up a plumb line as a standard in the midst of his people. (Isaiah 28:17 and Amos 7: 7-8).

Often times we seek a new measure of morality and uprightness based on our comfort. Sometimes the justification that we are looking for is found in the actions of others. Therefore, if someone is doing it, then it must be ok for me. As a result, I should not feel bad for that because others are doing the same thing. Hence the line just moved. If we continue on this path, we will literally no longer be under GOD.

Have you ever noticed that if one person gets the courage to do or say something, someone else will feel empowered to do or say the same thing? This can be seen as both good and bad. Have you ever found yourself looking for someone who feels or struggles with the same thing as you? Often times we get a sense of uprightness when we discover that our problems appear to be common or normal. The more people who are dealing with the same issue as ours makes us feel as if our problems are not issues at all. Another shift in our moral plumb line. This is why the LORD remains our standard because He does not change. It is important that we investigate these internal affairs utilizing the Word of GOD to reestablish our moral center. With GOD in mind, we should perform an internal audit evaluating our thoughts and actions to become more self-aware, identifying our chief complaint and past moral history. The Bible declares that if we confess our sins to GOD, he will be faithful and just to forgive us and to cleanse us of all unrighteousness. By using GOD's plumb line, we can self-identify where we have fallen short of GOD's glory. Allowing us to recognize that we are wrong, and He is right. As a result, leading us to a place of repentance. We must consistently activate our own Internal Affairs division. We should make routine self-assessments in order to investigate any suspicious behavior and conduct occurring within our soul. These routine internal investigations will help to ensure that abnormal behaviors or actions do not become intrinsic to who we are. These personal internal audits help to identify the source of our conflict and deal with it appropriately. The Apostle Paul stated if he continues to do that which he does not want to do, then he recognizes that it is no longer him but the sin dwelling and working in his flesh that is causing him to fall short of GOD's glory. He recognizes that his struggle is internal, and it is intrinsic to his carnal nature. That is why he was in a continuous process of putting off the old man and putting on the new man or walk in the new nature that is only found in Christ Jesus.

Most of us will go to the doctor when we realize that something is not functioning properly. During our visit, we have to tell the doctor our chief complaint as well as give them a history of the problem in order for them to attempt to provide a diagnosis. For us to provide the physician with a history of the complaint, we must be aware of what our normal is and when things became abnormal. Defining normal can be tricky, this is why we need an objective and consistent measuring tool. To a person that was born blind, walking in darkness is ordinary. However, because 20/20 vision is the plumb line we can distinguish good vision from bad. Our standard for vision helps us to understand being visually impaired is not normal. Some patients are so used to living with pain, and as a result, everyday discomfort is standard. However, we all know that it is not. As followers of Christ, we understand that the Word of GOD must be our plumb line measuring our everyday life. We are a work in progress, and without the use of an objective measuring tool, it is difficult to determine what is truly straight, upright, and just.

The Word of GOD is our plumb line for morality and righteousness. Jesus told his disciples if anyone or anything causes you to fall short of GOD's standard make a decision and separate yourself from it. Remove yourself from any source of temptation that is causing you to sway, resulting in a crooked line when compared to the line GOD has set. For it is better to enter heaven missing someone or something than to keep all that you have and be thrown into an everlasting fire (Matthew 5:29-30; Matthew 18:8-9). This is why we need to develop an Office of Internal Affairs in our soul to inspect the inner activities of our mind, will, and emotions. To ensure that systemic problems are fixed and problematic interior processes are removed or dealt with appropriately. As stated earlier, we need to make sure that our measuring tool is unbiased, objective and does not change; therefore, everyday life, as well as our personal character, must be based on standards that are outlined in the Word of GOD.

Internal affairs units are not exclusive to law enforcement, but they are seen in other types of businesses or agencies such as hospitals and pharmacies under the heading of risk management, human resources, or some other name. In this sense, the function of the internal affairs unit is not to condemn or enforce laws, but rather to audit and monitor activities, individuals or processes within the agency to identify and report violations of the laws or codes of conduct. The Office of Internal Affairs seeks to find the truth to what or why inner misconduct has occurred within the organization. It is amazing, but one function of our conscience is to serve as

our internal affairs division. Our consc
condemn us but rather identify and repor
moral standards to our heart and mind.
investigation, if our actions were off base, conviction ..
in causing us to feel guilty. As a result, our emotions take over
causing us to move or shift back into alignment with the Word
of GOD. One question that arises at this point is who
established our moral standards? The Bible declares that our
basic human uprightness or righteousness is not a good
standard to use. GOD compares our righteousness or justice to
a rag that a woman has used during her menstrual cycle (Isaiah
64:6). In many instances, moral values may vary from person
to person based on what we want or how we feel. In other
words, if there is something that we are struggling with in our
flesh instead of calling ourselves out or convicting ourselves
because of our wrong, we look for a way to justify what we have
done or what we are doing. As a result, we no longer feel bad
because what was once wrong in our own eyes in now right.
That is why we must use the Word of GOD as our standard for
moral virtue and righteousness. Only the creator can tell when
their product is not functioning according to specifications.

GOD asked Adam "who told you that you were naked?" At
that moment, the LORD knew that man was morally sick, and
he was not functioning appropriately. The LORD began an
investigation and interrogated the witness. Who told you?
Have you eaten? What have you done? It all went back to
Satan's suggestion "Did GOD really say?" Neither Adam nor
Eve did an internal investigation or inward inspection to

ertain where the desire to eat of the tree came from, they both just ate. The LORD did not judge them based on where the thought originated, but because of the action that was taken as a result of the thought. An inward investigation or audit can also give us insight into the policy itself that may have issues. All of us must develop a division of internal affairs within our soul (heart and mind). Our internal affairs unit should not condemn us or confer some sort of eternal and divine punishment, but rather convict us. Our conscience should show us where, and how we went off course allowing us the opportunity to make the appropriate changes in our lives. Our conscience reminds us that GOD is right, and the thing that we are doing that does not fall in line with His will, or His ways is wrong. Our thoughts should be GOD's thoughts, and our ways should be his ways. Jesus Christ died that we might be able to go back to the place where we were before sin entered and corrupted the nature of man.

DO YOU PROMISE TO KNOW THE WHOLE TRUTH?

John 8:32 (KJV)
And ye shall know the truth and the truth shall make you free.

The word "truth" is a noun (a word used to identify a person place, thing or idea). Truth is defined as 1) the quality or state of being true; 2) that which is true or in accordance with fact or reality; 3) a fact, belief, or idea that is accepted as true; 4) the state of being the case; the body of real things, events, and facts; 5) fidelity (faithful) to an original or to a standard. Based on the above definitions, to find the truth, we must identify the facts as well as identify that which is accepted as true. Gathering facts can be challenging because it is based on the observations of an individual or a group. Getting different individuals or groups to see the identical thing or see things the same way can be a difficult task. I can remember the craze going on in 2015 about "what color is the dress?" Some saw the color of the dress as being black with blue stripes, and some saw it as white with gold stripes. The question becomes, what is the truth based on? Is it based on the facts or is it based on what is accepted as true? One group believed strongly that the dress was black with blue stripes, and this was based on what they saw; therefore, their answer was the truth based on the facts. The other group saw it as white with gold stripes, and this was based on what they saw; as a result, their answer was the truth based on their facts. This leaves us with a major problem because the truth (absolute truth) cannot antagonize or conflict with itself. Therefore, there must be some facts that we do not see that is affecting what we do see as well as how we see.

Matthew 6:22-23 (KJV)
The light of the body is the eye: if therefore thine eye be single, thy whole body shall be full of light. Vs23 But if thine eye be evil, thy whole body shall be full of darkness. If therefore the light that is in thee be darkness, how great is that darkness!

Science teaches us that light enters the eye at distinctive wavelengths, and these wavelengths are matched to the different colors from the spectrum. When light hits the retina of the eye, neural signals are sent to the visual cortex which causes the brain to process those signals and transform them into an image. It is critical to note that the first rush of light that hits the retina is made of whatever wavelengths currently illuminating the room or environment and reflecting off the image you are looking at. Our brain figures out what color light is bouncing off the object that our eyes are viewing and essentially creates a copy of the image that we see. This happens all the time when we are getting dressed. A man can wear the same necktie; but, depending on the color of the shirt that he wears the necktie will look different. With all of this in mind, we should think about the dress controversy a little different. Now we understand that both groups saw what they saw; nevertheless, we do not know which group is looking at the dress in the correct light. In the way same that the light currently illuminating a room or an environment skews what we see, so does our current mindset, attitude, perception, or state of enlightenment affects what think about life as well as others.

It is amazing how something can look white until you compare it to something that is truly white. The converse is also true. I had a blue suit that was so dark most people thought it was black until I held it next to something, which was actually black. We must understand the light, the environment that we are in, and the angle or mindset which we are looking from will always affect what we see as well as how we see. In the book of Titus, the first chapter verse fifteen declares that to the pure all things are pure; however, unto them that are defiled and unbelieving is nothing pure. Even their mind and conscience are corrupted. The truth can only be determined in the presence of true light, from GOD's view and from GOD's mindset. The Psalm writer declared through GOD's precepts, he got an understanding, and that is the reason he hates lies. He also stated that GOD's word was a lamp to his feet and a light upon his path (Psalms 119:104-105). When conducting leadership training, I would have the participants draw a pyramid. I would then ask, from which angle would you have the best view? Of course, everyone would say from the top of the pyramid. Therefore, those in a position to see the different angles are able to construct a better opinion than those that can only see one-dimensionally. We often judge situations or people based solely on the information that we are given or the angle that we can see. Rarely do we weigh all the information as well as consider the source of information. We will never be able to see from the appropriate angle unless we look beyond ourselves.

Only from GOD's point of view can we see things from the appropriate angle. GOD told Job that He causes it to rain where there are no people (Job 38:26-27). To make this point even clearer, GOD asked Job "Do you know thou the time when the wild goats of the rock bring forth? Or do you watch as the deer give birth?" (Job 39:1 KJV). GOD makes it clear; in our existing state, we do not see what He sees because our light is not bright enough, and our point of view is not high enough. In our current physical, mental, and spiritual state of being, we cannot see what He sees, the way He sees it. Nor do we have the knowledge and wisdom to make the choices necessary. The Word of GOD declares that although we have eyes to see we do not see. Although, we have ears to hear we do not hear and what we hear we cannot understand. Oh, by the way; the centers of each rectangle are the same color.

2 Corinthians 4:3-6 (KJV)
But if our gospel be hid, it is hid to them that are lost: Vs4 In whom the god of this world hath blinded the minds of them which believe not, lest the light of the glorious gospel of Christ, who is the image of God, should shine unto them. Vs5 For we preach not ourselves, but Christ Jesus the Lord; and

ourselves your servants for Jesus' sake. Vs6 For God, who commanded the light to shine out of darkness, hath shined in our hearts, to give the light of the knowledge of the glory of God in the face of Jesus Christ.

You shall know the truth, and the truth shall make you free (John 8:32). GOD reveals the truth, and as a consequence of this revelation, we reach another level of enlightenment which brings freedom (psychological and spiritual). They say one sign of an addiction is denial, and the first step to recovery is admitting that there is a problem and the need for help. Many people do not realize that they have a problem; as a result, they are bound to make the same mistakes. This person is said to be in bondage or a slave to their problem. The Bible declares that you are a servant to whomever you submit yourself to; whether you become a servant to sin unto death, or you become a servant of obedience unto righteousness. Through obedience to the doctrine of Christ, we are made free from sin (Romans 6:16-18). Only when we are ready to receive revelation or accept the fact that we have a problem are we able to get on the path to freedom. Jesus stated healthy individuals have no need of a physician, but those that are sick have a need. Jesus also stated that he did not come to call the blameless, but offenders to repentance (Mark 2:17).

Outside of an annual check-up, no one goes to the doctor when they are healthy and feeling well. Many people die due to colon cancer because it goes undetected or unchecked for long periods. Some of the early warning signs (i.e., diarrhea, constipation, bloating, and abdominal discomfort) are present;

however, we see them as individual problems never putting the whole picture together. The patient may feel stomach pain, but an internal investigation would have identified the real problem as cancer. Although colorectal cancer is the third most common cancer in the United States, numerous patients decline the opportunity to have a colonoscopy performed. Many Individuals act irrationally declining (avoid) this exam due to emotions of fear, embarrassment, and disgust. The same is true with sin and our eternal salvation. The signs of sin and our need for a savior are there; however, many seemingly ignore the signs and symptoms that are manifesting. Numerous individuals often times reject the gospel of Christ and his offer of salvation because of those same emotions of fear and embarrassment. What do you do when someone offers you Christ? Do you really know that you are out of alignment with GOD's plumb line? Most do not until they are almost at the point of death and there appears to be no hope. The good news is that in GOD, there is always hope.

Nevertheless, if you do not realize or receive the revelation of who you are and what you need, you will never make the changes that are necessary to become the person GOD has called you to be. In the book of Acts, the second chapter Peter is declaring the gospel of Christ, and then something happened. The Bible states that when they heard what Peter was teaching, they were pricked in their hearts (thoughts, feelings, and mind) and asked what they should do? Peter responded and said, repent and be baptized in the name of Jesus Christ for the remission of your sins. Question, why would you repent or ask for forgiveness if you haven't done anything wrong? They must have had a revelation that they were sick; there was something in their nose; that they have sinned and have come short of the glory of GOD.

Truth causes us to walk in freedom, and true freedom begins with our state of mind. A partial truth only brings partial freedom causing a person to think more highly of himself than he ought to think. A partial truth is only a part of the big picture. It can be the beginning of growth and maturity, but it can also be the basis for a well-developed lie and deception. Our enemy, the devil, does not want us to come into the knowledge of the truth. Not full knowledge anyway, because a person that fully understands the big picture (the whole truth) is not easily deceived nor denied what rightfully belongs to them. A person who is void of the truth and spiritual understanding is like a child or one who is inexperienced and is easily led astray. Ephesians the fourth chapter verses thirteen and fourteen says once we come together in the unity of our faith, and in the knowledge of the Son of God, we will become completely matured in GOD, measuring up to the full maturity of Christ. Once we reach that place in our faith and knowledge of Jesus, we will no longer be immature acting like children that are easily influenced and blown around by every wind of doctrine, by individuals who try to deceive.

If we do develop a firm foundation and grow in the truth of GOD's word, we will no longer be vulnerable and open to every whim of Satan's deceptions. Satan wants to use our lack of understanding regarding the entire truth against us to confuse, frustrate, deceive, and ultimately lead us astray. A partial truth in the hands of the enemy is a powerful tool when used against the young and immature Christian mind. In the temptation of Christ, Satan tries to use the truth of GOD's word against Christ. In Matthew chapter four verse six Satan said to Jesus "if you are the Son of GOD, throw yourself down; for it is written, He (GOD) will give his angels charge over you, and they will bear you up in their hands, lest you dash your foot against a stone." In this passage, Satan wanted to use the truth of GOD's Word deceitfully (2 Corinthians 4:2) to lead Christ astray and cause him (Christ) to fall short of the will of GOD for his life. We must remember a misplaced truth can be a well-placed lie. Christ's full knowledge of the Scriptures allowed him to recognize that Satan was speaking a truth; however, not in the appropriate context. Yes, the WORD of GOD does say that he would give His angels charge over us and they will bear us up in their hands, lest we dash our feet against a stone. At the same time, that does not mean that we are to deliberately place ourselves in harm's way just to see if He (GOD) will do what He said. GOD forbid! Remember, GOD also commands us not to tempt Him. The second point to this temptation seen in Matthew four verse six is that Satan wants Jesus to question who he is in GOD. Satan used this same tactic against Woman (now called Eve) in the Garden of Eden.

In Genesis, three verse five Satan tells the woman that GOD knows after you eat from the tree of the knowledge of good and evil your eyes will be opened, which is a truth. However, eating from the tree would not make them like gods because they were already gods upon the earth. When God decided to form man, God's purpose was to have man function like Him in the earth. That is why He made man in His image and after His likeness and gave man dominion over the fish of the sea, and over the fowl of the air, and over every living thing that moves upon the earth (Genesis 1:26-28). Luke chapter four verses five and six states that the devil took Jesus up into a high mountain, showed him all the kingdoms of the world in a moment of time. And Satan said unto Jesus, all this power will I give thee, and the glory of them: for they have been delivered unto me; and to whomsoever, I will I give it. Again, it is true Adam did deliver his power and his right to rule this world to Satan, allowing him (Satan) to become the god of this world (2 Corinthians 4:4). However, Jesus' purpose was to overthrow Satan, not worship him. The Creator (GOD) called on Jesus to destroy the works of the devil, not to submit to them. Satan tried to get Christ to settle for a little temporary power and glory when all power and everlasting glory already belonged to Christ.

A misplaced truth can make a well-placed lie believable. When I was in high school, one of my teachers played a joke on me. The class had taken an exam, and as I was turning in my exam, I stated, "I know that's an A." The teacher was passing the exams back, and I knew that I did well; however, when I got my exam, I saw that I had a low score. I looked at the first page and said, "this is not my paper," but when I looked on the next page it was. Initially, I was adamant that was not my paper, but the more I looked upon the truth (the 2nd page) with the lie, the more I became unsure. I began to doubt and say maybe I didn't do as well as I thought. She laughed and pulled out my first page so that I could see my true score. It is amazing how part truth caused me to believe what I knew was not true.

Genesis 27:22-27 (KJV)
And Jacob went near unto Isaac, his father; and he felt him, and said, The voice is Jacob's voice, but the hands are the hands of Esau. vs23 And he discerned him not, because his hands were hairy, as his brother Esau's hands: so he blessed him. vs24 And he said, Art thou my very son Esau? And he said I am. vs25 And he said, Bring it near to me, and I will eat of my son's venison, that my soul may bless thee. And he brought it near to him, and he did eat: and he brought him wine, and he drank. vs26 And his father Isaac said unto him, Come near now, and kiss me, my son. vs27 And he came near, and kissed him: and he smelled the smell of his raiment, and blessed him, and said, See, the smell of my son is as the smell of a field which the LORD hath blessed:

In the scripture above Isaac realized that the voice seemed false; however, the hands and the smell seemed true. As a result, Isaac blessed Jacob and not his oldest son Esau. It is amazing how our mind works to accept or reject information. Even when we know that some aspect of the information appears to be false, our minds will block or hide the inaccurate information from our conscious mind if there is enough information that appears to be accurate. As a result, we are deceived because we only focus on the part that we believe to be true and not all of the information that is presented. Isaac knew the voice that he heard was not Esau's, but he still blessed Jacob because he believed the hands and the smell were Esau. Our desire to trust people can hinder us from looking at all the information. Could it have been possible that Isaac desired to trust Jacob; therefore, he would not believe that Jacob would trick him? He heard Jacob's voice, but he was not sure if Jacob would deceive him. Also, our lack of trust in ourselves or our abilities can hinder us from looking at all the information. Isaac did not trust himself because his senses were failing. Isaac's age and his inability to see with his eyes caused him to doubt what he heard with his ears. Jacob's ability to mix true characteristics of Esau with his own voice caused Isaac to believe a part truth instead of knowing the whole truth.

How many times have you heard check your source? I think we all may know someone that would tell stories that seemed true, but the story was more lie than the truth. If you repeated what you heard to someone else, they would ask, who told you that? Once you tell them, their next comment might be "You know you can't believe half of what they say." This is why we must learn not to focus on the parts that seem true, but rather evaluate all the information so that you could determine if the story is true or not. Deuteronomy chapter four verse two admonishes us not to add to the Word of GOD attempting to strengthen it nor take anything away from the Word of GOD in an attempt to weaken it. When we are talking or witnessing to someone about GOD, we do not have to add to the Word to make it seem more believable, and we cannot take away or leave out something in an attempt to make it easier for others to receive and not be offended. The truth can appear exciting, but it also can appear dull. The truth can be peaceful, but it also can be offensive. No matter how the truth sounds or makes us feel, if we repeat exactly what happened or if we say what GOD said, the truth will always be true and effective. So, I ask you again. Do you promise to know the truth, the whole truth and nothing but the truth so help you, GOD?

To know the truth, we must listen and receive the Word of GOD. According to Romans chapter ten verse seventeen, faith comes by hearing what is preached or told from the Word of GOD. That is true, but it is not the whole truth when we focus on hearing only. The disciples of John the Baptist came to Jesus asking are you the one or should we look for another? Jesus' response was, go and tell John again the things which you hear and see. Jesus also told Philip that if he cannot believe based on what you have heard me say than believe because of what you have seen me do. Please realize, that it is not what you hear alone that builds your faith, but rather it is what you hear, see, and understand that builds your faith. To take this a little further, the Bible declared that you shall know the truth and the truth shall liberate you free (John 8:32). To know the truth is to be able to clearly express, perceive, and understand. Knowing the truth means to be sure of something. Thus, it is not only the amount of truth you hear that brings freedom, but rather it is the amount of truth you hear, understand, and are able to clearly express with surety that brings freedom. How can you walk in, receive, or apply the truth if you do not understand what you have heard?

The gospel of Matthew the thirteenth chapter verses thirteen through nineteen deals with the necessity of understanding what you hear. Verse nineteen tell us that anyone who does not understand the truth that they hear is the same as a person who received seed by the wayside and the evil one comes and snatches away the seed (Word) that was sown. To understand is to grasp, appreciate, know, comprehend, recognize, be aware of, value, and identify with. As a professor, I try to get my students to understand the basic principles before I go into deeper issues. However, the challenge is getting them to understand, appreciate, comprehend or ultimately value the basics, especially when these principles seem so different from the subject matter they feel they need to know. Often times individuals try to determine what they should be learning when they don't know what they need to know. Our desire to know can interfere with our ability to understand and learn. Rudimentary addition and subtraction seem so different from algebra; however, basic addition and subtraction are the foundation of algebra. A person's preconceived notion concerning algebra can inhibit their ability to receive and ultimately understand any teaching on the foundations of algebra. If you do not value basic math, it will be difficult for you to grasp or gain an understanding of algebra let alone calculus.

Can we really understand what it means to be saved if we did not learn what it means to repent of our sins or have faith in GOD? How can we understand repentance if we have not learned about sin or what is sin? The Bible tells us that if we confess our sins to GOD, He will be faithful and just to forgive us of our sins and cleanse us of all unrighteousness, but why confess and repent for something that we do not believe is a sin. It is amazing how many people want to learn about prophecy or about casting out devils, but they do not have a clear understanding of salvation. We are quick to submit to a prophecy, but we have a hard time receiving and submitting to sound doctrine. Sound doctrine is at the foundation of understanding and receiving true prophecy. The basics are the foundations or the keys to understanding and understanding is the key to knowing the whole truth. Understanding is not a prerequisite to obey GOD; however, it is a prerequisite to mature in GOD. Remember wisdom and knowledge in the hands of a fool is foolishness. Understanding comes from developing a relationship with someone or something. If two people understood each other some may say that they are able to see things from each other's point of view.

True relationship (connection, rapport, and bond) comes from frequency and repetition of communication or interaction. Another word for communication and interaction is intercourse, not sex. Sexual intercourse most times happens as a result of frequent communication or interaction. Question, how often do you spend time with GOD? How often do you communicate with Him through his Word and prayer?

To know the truth means to develop a relationship, bond, or connection through frequent communication. It means to become intimate with as to cause to give birth. Our understanding of the Word of GOD must be like a seed being planted in the womb of our heart (mind, soul) causing us to become pregnant and ultimately to give birth or bring forth the manifestation of GOD's will for our life and this world. This relationship does not come by reading the Word once or talking to GOD every now and then, but it comes from a consistent reading and praying (consistent intercourse – communicating and interacting with GOD and His Word). Through relationship, GOD begins to reveal the hidden mysteries of His Word. Men have studied the bible for centuries and have not come to the fullness of the truth. GOD's Word can be studied, but the ultimate truth has to be revealed.

Proverbs chapter twenty-five verse two states that it is the glory of God to camouflage or hide a thing, but the honor of kings is to penetrate and to examine intimately in order to search out and discover the truth. In the book of first Corinthians chapter two, the Apostle Paul states that we speak wisdom that can only be understood by those that are matured in GOD. Those that are full of worldly wisdom cannot understand the wisdom of GOD and they do not see the whole truth. If the princes of this world truly understood the wisdom of GOD and the whole truth about the Word of GOD they would not have crucified Jesus our LORD and Savior. The whole truth is like putting up a billboard. Billboards are put together section by section until the whole picture is clear. When preaching the gospel, we teach truth by truth until the whole truth is made clear. One aspect or one scripture from the Bible is true but it is not the whole truth when left alone, and it is not true at all when taken out of context. All have sinned, but there is GOD's grace. GOD is plenteous in mercy, but He is a GOD of wrath and judgment. I write these things that you sin not, but if you do sin, you have an advocate. However, shall we continue in sin that grace may abound? GOD forbid! There is an old poem about six blind men that touched different parts of an elephant and as a result, came up with different truths. They were partly right and yet to be partially right is to be all wrong. Based on their assessment, they all developed differences of opinions. These part truths resulted in each of them becoming firmer in their beliefs as they argued with each other. First Corinthians the thirteenth chapter verses nine and ten teaches us that in our current place of understanding we know in part and we prophesy in part. However, when that which is complete comes, then those things which are incomplete shall be done away. This is why we must promise to know the whole truth.

1Corinthians 2:4-8 (KJV)

And my speech and my preaching was not with enticing words of man's wisdom, but in demonstration of the Spirit and of power: Vs5 That your faith should not stand in the wisdom of men, but in the power of God. Vs6 Howbeit we speak wisdom among them that are perfect: yet not the wisdom of this world, nor of the princes of this world, that come to nought: Vs7 But we speak the wisdom of God in a mystery, even the hidden wisdom, which God ordained before the world unto our glory: Vs8 Which none of the princes of this world knew: for had they known it, they would not have crucified the Lord of glory.

BEWARE OF PROGRESSIVE TRUTH

In today's society, it is very important that we are able to distinguish the truth from a lie. Nowadays, information is everywhere, and it is readily and easily accessible. All you have to do is type or say what you want to know, and in seconds you will have thousands of options to choose from. The problem is that some sources may say, interpret, or define information different from another. What do we do? Who do we believe? The Word of GOD admonishes us not to believe every person speaking or teaching but rather try their heart and inner thoughts as well as the spirit that is speaking through them to see whether they are from GOD or not (1John 4:1). The Bible also tells us that many people have forsaken the truth of GOD's Word and given attention to seducing spirits and doctrines of devils. These individuals secretly and progressively introduce destructive heresies as if they were the gospel truth. These corrupt and liberal teachings are designed to debase the moral and spiritual standards of truth within the Word GOD, and anyone who declares the way of truth will be smeared/maligned. In this day of gain, greed, incontinence, and selfish ambition many in society have developed a form of godliness, but their basic beliefs are in rebellion to GOD and deny the very existence of His power. Today many individuals handle the Word of GOD deceitfully in an attempt to deceive and exploit others as well as to make them feel good or encourage their current lifestyle.

2Peter 2:1-3 (ISV)
Now there were false prophets among the people, just as there also will be false teachers among you, who will secretly introduce destructive heresies and even deny the Master who bought them, bringing swift destruction on themselves. Vs2 Many people will follow their immoral ways, and because of them the way of truth will be maligned. Vs3 In their greed they will exploit you with deceptive words. The ancient verdict against them is still in force, and their destruction is not delayed.

Many will quote the Word of GOD, but their intent in the eyes of the LORD is ungodly. As discussed earlier, even Satan quoted Scripture in an attempt to entice Jesus to sin. Satan said to Jesus, if you are the Son of GOD, throw yourself down from the pinnacle of this temple; because it is written (Matthew 4:6, Luke 4:10-11, Psalms 91: 11-12). You see Satan took the Scriptures and tried to formulate a new truth. The issue is not with what Satan said, but rather it was the wrong intent behind what was said. We understand that the meaning of a statement is not solely determined by the definitions of the words used but by the intent and tone in which they are being said. As discussed before Jesus knew more than how to quote the scriptures, He understood what the scriptures meant (the intent). He knew the whole truth. Christ taught his disciples that anyone who heard the Word of the kingdom but did not understand it, the enemy would come to take away that which was sown in his heart. The evil one cannot stop the word from being spoken but he can affect or rather infect the how the word is spoken and our inability to understand what is being said; as a consequence, the word would not take root. The Scriptures declare that GOD's people are destroyed because of their lack of knowledge (Hosea 4:6). Satan's progressive or liberal interpretation of the Scripture was designed to cause Jesus to ignorantly disobey the will of GOD all the while thinking that he is walking in accordance with the Holy Scriptures.

Have you ever heard the saying "Ignorance Kills"? Ignorance is defined as not knowing something due to a lack of information or intelligence. Ignorance also may be defined as not understanding or ignoring the information that is presented. Hence ignorant individuals are usually referred to as uneducated, unlearned, uninformed, or unenlightened. Progressive teachings that bring forth an action or change have identified a level of ignorance and are attempting to fill in the gaps. The word progressive also implies that this change or action is occurring gradually. For example; years ago, we knew that the earth was flat, but as knowledge has progressed, and we have a greater understanding; we now know that the earth is round. Let's look at a different example. You and I are close friends, and most times when you see me, I am wearing something that is orange and green with the name of my alma mater or its mascot. You would assume that orange and green are my favorite colors because they are the most common colors that I wear. So, we are on a game show, and it is time for the final question. I have my answer already written down. They ask you "what are my favorite colors"? You are so excited because you know the answer. I am excited as well because I think that you know me and we are going to win. You shout out loud and proud "orange and green." My smile turns to a frown as I turn the card over to reveal my answer, "black and gold." You assumed, but we never talked about my favorite colors. Although, we did not win this situation presented an opportunity for you to know my ways and not just my actions (your knowledge grew or progressed). Yes, I wear orange and green because I love my alma mater, but my favorite colors are black and gold.

What if I told you directly that my favorite colors are orange and green; however, on the show, I wrote black, and gold are my favorite colors? How would you feel? Would you feel that you learned something new about your friend or would feel that your friend lied? In the first example, the truth maintained fidelity with the original standard; although, it was an assumption based on the frequentness of wearing the colors. You are correct, I do wear a lot of orange and green, but it is not for the love of the colors but rather the love for the university. You now have a better understanding of why. In the second example, the truth completely changed. You made your response based on the fact of what I told you, and for some reason the facts have changed. What if I said, "I have the right to change my mind"? Some people may think that GOD changed His truth when He instituted the New Covenant. However, when we take a deeper look, we see that the New

Testament was already in GOD's plan. Galatians the third chapter declares that the Scripture, knowing beforehand that God would justify and proclaim righteous the Gentiles by faith, GOD preached, declaring the good news of the coming Savior to Abraham well in advance of the gospel.

The book of Galatians also tells us that before faith came, we were kept under the Law. GOD used the Law to serve as our disciplinarian and tutor, one who was entrusted with the responsibility of leading and guiding us to Christ. The Law had to be stern and severe in its punishments as it was responsible for our safety and conduct. The LORD used the law to prepare the way for faith in Christ by producing convictions of guilt and helplessness (Galatians 3:8-25). The Apostle Paul acknowledged that if it had not been for the Law, he would not have been aware of sin or have known its meaning. He goes on to say that he would not have had consciousness and a sense of guilt concerning covetousness if the Law had not repeatedly said, do not covet. You see, by the Holy Spirit we are able to gain a greater understanding and discover the mysteries of GOD that are hidden in His Word; however, His truth does not change. Satan uses progressive truth as a means to change the true meaning of the original statement. Christ is the lamb that was slain from the foundation of the world. Psalm one-hundred-three verse seven declares that GOD made known his ways to Moses and His acts to the children of Israel. Israel saw what the LORD did, but Moses understood why. Question, are you getting to know the character of GOD or his actions? The matured believer begins to understand the ways of GOD and are not easily deceived unlike those that only know His actions. Do not allow the enemy to explain GOD's actions utilizing progressive truths that lead us away from GOD's original standard and reason for why.

In a progressive society, would it be okay for the truth to change based on how we feel or what we are willing to publish and accept as true? We must be cautious of liberal truth that disguises itself as a new revelation. Wherever there is a lack of knowledge, there is an opportunity for the truth to progress. Also, it must be said that wherever there is ignorance, it is much easier to change or move the truth from its original standard to something that is accepted as true and published as truth. By slowly introducing new information, what was once thought of as fact may be looked upon as false.

Let's pause for a second and think about this, because we do not truly understand where all the people of the earth came from there is room for speculation. This speculation by researchers is called a hypothesis or an educated guess. This hypothesis (theory) is the basis for an investigation/research that is designed to target this ignorance and provide answers to the questions that have been formulated. The data gathered from the investigation is used to fill in the gaps in our knowledge, and it becomes the foundation of what we would accept as true. Even if one-hundred percent of the data does not say the same thing or does not agree with what is hypothesized, its results can be used to argue in favor of the educated guess. Wow, an educated guess with limited data can be seen as true, and this information becomes the foundation in which other truths are built upon. For example; some scientists have speculated that life began randomly as a single cell organism and evolved over billions of years to become apes and then ultimately humans. For this to be true, the Earth must be dated, and it must be billions of years old for the evolution theory to hold true.

Many believe that early human life began in Africa and dispersed abroad as they evolved. This belief gives rise to the notion that one group (race) of humans are more evolved than others. We must understand that many racist individuals ignorantly believe that their race is more evolved or higher up on the tree of evolution. Hence, some believe that all humans evolved from apes; with people of color being closer to the apes; while white people are the higher and more evolved of the species. As Christians, we believe in creation and a divine creator. We have faith in the Bible which tells us that in the beginning GOD created Adam and Woman (for she was not called Eve until after man sinned) and from them, all the generations of man began. If we believe this, then we must believe that all nations and skin tones stemmed from Adam and Woman in the beginning. Also, when reading in the book of Genesis chapters ten and eleven we see that after the flood, the earth was repopulated with the descendants of one man (Noah).

In Scripture, we see that when GOD wanted to separate the children of man he did not do it by changing skin tone but by changing their language. In Genesis, the eleventh chapter the Bible declares that there was a time when everyone on the entire earth spoke a common language with an identical dialect. The people said amongst themselves, let us build a city for ourselves, and a tower whose top will reach into the heavens, and let us make a name for ourselves so that we will not be scattered and dispersed over the face of the entire earth as the LORD GOD had instructed. And the LORD said the people are unified. They are living and working together as one single group for they all have the same language. What they are attempting to accomplish now (in rebellion) is only the beginning of what they can achieve, and nothing is impossible for them because they are one people with one language. Anything they can imagine to do, they can do it. Because of this GOD mixed up and confused their language so that they could not communicate with or understand one another.

The Bible reveals that it was their inability to comprehend what each other was saying that caused them to become disjointed and scattered upon the face of all the earth. The color of their skin or outward appearance had nothing to do with their being detached and separated from each other. Christ died that we might be reconciled and live together as one in GOD and yet we choose to separate based on color. Remember, the lack of knowledge is a point of entry for progressive truth. GOD did not intend for us to be separated based on our color/skin tone but by our inability to communicate. If we think about it, every region has its own language and dialect. I had a roommate in college, his parents were Jamaican; however, he was born and raised in England until he was a teenager. Although his parents had a Jamaican accent, his accent was British. I have seen people that looked Asian, yet they talked with a Jamaican tongue. You see people of a common language tend to migrate to similar geographic regions. This geographic region then can affect the language and dialect that is spoken. The Bible declares in Genesis the tenth chapter that the people were dispersed after their tongues, in their lands, after their nations were the families of the sons of Noah divided throughout the earth after the flood (Genesis 10:31-32). The Word of GOD also states that GOD made every nation of humanity from one man (from one common origin, one source, one blood) and caused them to settle all over the face of the earth, having determined their allotted periods of time and having fixed the national boundaries and territories within which they live (Acts 17:26). The color of their skin never played a part in how they were to be separated. Racism is derived from a progressive idea that is often rooted in some aspect of evolution, and it is an aberration from GOD's original standard. Again, racism is an example of how an educated (uneducated) guess with limited data can be seen as true, and this information becomes the foundation in which other false truths are built upon.

A Progressive may be defined as a person advocating or implementing social reform or new, liberal ideas. In an attempt to become more progressive or liberal, many people are willing to do away with human biology as well as human anatomy and physiology as a means to distinguish between male and female. The Bible declares that after GOD made man He said that it is not good for him to be alone; therefore, I will make for him a helper, a counterpart suitable for him. This is amazing because after The LORD made that statement, the Bible declares that the LORD GOD caused all the animals of the earth to pass before Adam to see what he would call them. The second chapter of Genesis states that the LORD GOD formed out of the ground every beast of the field and every fowl of the air, and brought them to Adam to see what he would call them; and whatever he called any creature, that was its name. The Scriptures goes on to say that after Adam gave names to all of the livestock and birds that he did not find a suitable companion (help meet) or counterpart adapted for him (Genesis 2: 18-20). It appears as if Adam was looking for something that he did not find. It was as if GOD was waiting to see if Adam would be satisfied with something less appropriate (I am glad that Adam did not mess that up). GOD then causes Adam to fall into a deep sleep and performs the first surgery ever recorded. GOD makes the woman, and then He does the same thing that He did with the animals of the field and the birds of the air. He caused the woman to pass before man to see what he would call her. And Adam said, now she is bone of my bones, and flesh of my flesh: she shall be called Woman because she was taken out of Man and she is a complementary helper. Therefore, shall a man leave his father and his mother, and shall cling to his wife. Adam called the woman his wife.

If Adam did not want a woman (female) to be his wife, he could have easily called her something else, but he knew that SHE was it. Only a male and his female counterpart can come together and reproduce. Question, what kind of truth do we have if we feel that someone that has a different skin tone is less than human and yet a person born with male genitalia can be called a female because that is what he wants to be? If a white person wakes up one day and says that they are black, what would happen? Can a Black person wake up one day and say that I am a white person trapped in dark skin; therefore, they change all of their documents to say that they are white. We would not allow it, and we would say they have falsified their documents. Our society has stripped a white female and discredited all of her work because she identified with being black and yet we will give credit and support to a male that identifies with being a female and vice versa. We then allow them to confuse our children, teaching against being gender specific (discrediting human anatomy and physiology) and telling our children to call a male Ms. or Mx. Beware of progressive truths that move us away from the fidelity of the original standard that is set by GOD. We must be careful not to allow GOD's truth to be infused with Satan's lies.

Years ago, the civil right movement was about African Americans being able to receive their inalienable rights; legal rights that other Americans already held. As time has moved on, we now see a homosexual (LGTBQ) movement attaching their desires to the civil rights movement; as a result, while we continue to fight for civil liberties, we find ourselves fighting for the rights of actions that totally go against what we are supposed to believe as Christians. We cannot choose the color of our skin, but we can choose when and who we have sex with. I find that homosexuals are quick to tell a Black person "you of all people should understand what it is like to be discriminated against." That statement is true, but they are saying this in an attempt to gain support for their liberal lifestyle that contradicts the Word of GOD.

Some would say that Christians think they are better than everyone else, but the contrary is true. The Scriptures tell us that we all have sinned and fallen short of the glory of GOD. We did nothing to earn or deserve salvation; it was a gift extended to us from GOD. The Bible declares that there is only one who is the essence of perfection in every way and that is GOD. We are admonished not to think of ourselves more highly than we ought to think, but we are cautioned to analyze carefully and test our personal conduct. We are to perform an internal investigation without resorting to comparing ourselves with someone else whose struggles appear to be more obvious than our own. I think that everyone has an area of struggle in their life (the believer as well as the non-believer) and fornication and adultery are sins just as homosexuality. Chapter twelve in the book of Hebrews admonishes everyone to lay aside every weight and the sin that does so easily overcome and entangles us. That is why we must confess our sins and GOD is faithful and just to forgive us and cleanse us of all our unrighteousness. For the time is coming for the judgment of GOD to begin and this judgment will start first with the household of faith (the body of Christ). And if the righteous (having faith in Christ) are narrowly saved, what will be the consequence for them that do not obey the gospel of God (1 Peter 4: 17-18)?

Ezekiel 36:29-32
I will also save you from all your uncleannesses: and I will call for the corn, and will increase it, and lay no famine upon you. Vs30 And I will multiply the fruit of the tree, and the increase of the field, that ye shall receive no more reproach of famine among the heathen. Vs31 Then shall ye remember your own evil ways, and your doings that were not good, and shall lothe yourselves in your own sight for your iniquities and for your abominations. Vs32 Not for your sakes do I this, saith the Lord GOD, be it known unto you: be ashamed and confounded for your own ways, O house of Israel.

Progressive truths that stray from GOD's original standard do not lead to repentance but are designed to advocate for reform and acceptance. Liberal truths work to change GOD's standards and not to change our hearts and actions. Remember, we all must confess our sins and repent. Please understand, that the Bible tell us to love our neighbors as we love ourselves. The LORD has declared that with love and kindness He is beckoning all of us. I believe that everyone should be treated fairly and with dignity regardless of their race, religion, national origin, or sexual orientation. As Christians, we must remember that we all came to GOD in our own time and we must allow others the opportunity to do the same. It is our responsibility to continue to lovingly work with them praying that they come to GOD with a repented heart before it is too late. We must understand that our disagreement concerning what is considered sin should not be equated to or treated as if it is disdain or hatred towards someone else. The Bible tells us that a good father disciplines those he loves.

The scriptures also remind us of the fact that in a way that iron sharpens iron, so does one man sharpens and impacts another through their consistent discussion. If your best friend disagrees with your attitude or actions do you automatically say that he/she is spewing hate? GOD hates the sin, but He loves the person even though they may be entangled in sin. All He asks is for us to acknowledge that we have and still do sin. The Bible declares that the LORD is not delaying the promise of His return because He is slow or unable to perform. But He is being extraordinarily patient with us, not wishing for any of us to perish but for all us to come to repentance. With all of this in mind, sin is still sin, and as believers, we cannot lower our standards of faith to make ourselves or anyone else feel better about their lifestyle. The Word of GOD warns us that the time will come when people will not endure (tolerate) sound and accurate instruction that challenges and provokes them to grow in alignment with GOD's truth; but they will surround themselves with teachers that will speak soothing words that will satisfy their carnal desires and to support their errors (2Timothy 4:3).

The Scriptures declare that the prophets of Jerusalem were doing a terrible thing because they were unfaithful to GOD's commands and they were living a lie. The prophets were supporting and strengthening the hands of those who committed wicked acts so that no one would feel remorseful for their sinful actions and as a result, the people did not feel it was necessary for them to repent. The Scripture goes on to say that if prophets would have stood in place of intimacy with GOD and if they would have caused the people to hear His words, then they should have turned the people from their evil ways, and from the evil of their doings (Jeremiah 23:14-22).

The good and bad of progressive truth is that it can bring to light GOD's mysteries that have been hidden in His Word; however, it can also be a powerful tool used to introduce heresy and doctrines of devils. Remember that Ignorance may be defined as not understanding or ignoring information that is presented. Question, how many us feel like we truly understand all of the Scriptures and the intent for which they were written? Remember the enemy uses progressive truths to target the varying degrees of ignorance found within the Church. This is important to understand because many of us as believers appear to be uneducated and uncertain when it is time to communicate the things of GOD. Most of us are satisfied with being a child or a servant, while GOD wants us to mature and become sons.

The Bible tells us that the spiritually immature are easily influenced by false doctrines and deceitful people, and as a result, they are confused, not knowing what to believe (Ephesians 4:14). One person says this and another says that; what do I believe? For example, the Bible tells us to speak the truth in love that we may grow up becoming one with Christ;

however, often times if you tell someone the truth about themselves or their actions they would get upset and may say that you are judgmental and that is not demonstrating the love of GOD. Have you ever heard someone say that "Christians are judgmental"? As a result, many believers will say "I try not to judge" or "judge not lest ye be judged." Many will ignore the fact that the Bible also tells us to hold fast the profession of our faith without wavering. It also tells us to thoughtfully consider how to encourage, motivate and provoke each other unto love and to good works (Hebrews 10:23-24). We must understand, the truth itself judges us because it challenges us to grow. Most of us like words of praise and encouragement, but we are bothered by corrective criticism. Question, do we withhold correction or do we find a loving way, to tell the truth?

We have been discussing the pros and cons of progressive truth so, let me ask this question again; "what is truth"? Remember the word truth is a noun that can be defined as a fact, belief, or idea that is accepted as true. It can also be defined as something that maintains fidelity to an original standard. In the early to mid-eighties physicians had little knowledge about HIV/AIDS and now our knowledge has progressed so much so that what was once considered a death sentence may one day be prevented by the use of a vaccine. In the area of healthcare, we often find that what we thought was true years ago concerning some diseases was based on the limited knowledge of the disease itself at that time. As a result, the answer that was correct yesterday may be considered wrong as time progresses and our knowledge increases. In life, there are so many areas where we are ignorant, and we are continuously looking to advance. In some cases, as our knowledge expands, we realize that what we once thought as true is actually far from it. Who would have thought that the earth was round? As stated earlier, for years scientist knew that the world was flat; however, we now realize that their initial thoughts were totally wrong.

Scientific advancements may at times appear to have taken us away from what was once considered our original truth. This is also true when it comes to interpreting the Holy Scriptures. Before Christ, salvation was based on the works of the Law and now we understand that salvation rooted and grounded on faith in Christ. There are so many areas where we are continuously looking to increase our understanding and knowledge of GOD and His Word. However, while on this quest, we must understand that it is vitally important that the truth maintains fidelity to the original standard. This is why we use the Word of GOD to interpret the Word of GOD. We are taught to draw out the truth from a text in accordance with the context and its original meaning (exegesis) and not to impose our personal interpretation into or onto the text. When studying the Word of GOD, we must be careful not to interpret the text by reading our own ideas, feelings, and connotations into it (Eisegesis). In other words, do not be adulterous (unfaithful) to the original intent of the WORD.

I am so glad that the Church has progressed from living by works to living by faith. In the Old Testament relationship with GOD was based on works of the law, but in the New Testament our salvation is a gift from GOD. As as result, we can receive salvation by faith. Many in the early Church struggled with this seemingly new revelation of the truth because it seemed to be too progressive and was moving away from the original truth of GOD's Word. This is why we use scripture to interpret scripture. As we grow in the Word of GOD, we can see the salvation brought on by the life, death, burial, and resurrection of Jesus Christ throughout the Old and New Testaments. The story of Christ was concealed in the Old Testament and now is revealed in the New. Although, the truth was presented as a mystery in the Old Testament the story of Christ was still present. Therefore, the New Testament truth does not contradict the Old Testament scriptures concerning Christ. Christ declared that he did not come to destroy the law but to fulfill it.

Christ declared that all the things written in the Law of Moses and in the writings of the prophets, and in the Psalms concerning him had to be fulfilled (Luke 24:27, 44-45). Christ had to open the minds of his disciples for them to understand the Scriptures. The point of Christ dying for our sins and the fact that we are now saved by grace and not of works may appear to be progressive; however, these facts maintains fidelity to the original intent of GOD's Word. The Word of GOD is our original standard. As stated before, the Apostle Paul wrote to the Ephesians regarding the dispensation of grace and how GOD by revelation expounded upon the mystery of the Holy Scriptures which in earlier times was not made known unto the sons of men, as it is now revealed unto his apostles and prophets by the Holy Spirit (Ephesians 3: 2-5). Although this truth seemed to be progressive, it maintained fidelity to the original intent of the Word of GOD. The Spirit of GOD used the original scriptures to explain without changing the context or the meaning of the Scriptures. The Holy Spirit allowed Philip to use the writings of the prophet Isaiah teach the Ethiopian Eunuch good news about Jesus (Acts 8:26-39)

Isaiah 48:5-8 (AMP)
I have declared them to you long ago; Before they came to pass I announced them to you, So that you could not say, 'My idol has done them, And my carved image and my cast image have commanded them.' Vs6 "You have heard [these things foretold]; look at all this [that has been fulfilled]. And you, will you not declare it? I proclaim to you [specific] new things from this time, Even hidden things which you have not known. Vs7 "They are created now [called into being by the prophetic word] and not long ago; And before today you have not heard of them, So that you will not say, 'Oh yes! I knew them.' Vs8 "You have not heard, you have not known; Even from long ago your ear has not been open. For I [the LORD] knew that you [Israel] would act very treacherously; You have been called a transgressor and a rebel from birth.

It is amazing how things can change over time. Changes can occur due to a variety of reasons. Some changes are necessary and may be due to the fact that the old is broken, or we have more knowledge, revelation, and insight than in previous years. As our knowledge about engines, accidents, fuel, and our environment continues to progress it becomes increasingly necessary that the types of vehicles that are manufactured evolve as well. Years ago, fuel contained lead and cars were not fuel efficient. However, today's gasoline is lead-free and vehicles are more fuel efficient, if they use fuel at all. The Apostle Paul declared to the Ephesians that GOD had given him the grace to know and understand the hidden mysteries of Christ which in other ages these mysteries were not made known unto man. This change or increase in revelation is not because the old way was wrong or incorrect, but rather it was time. As stated earlier, the gospel of Christ was hidden in the Old Testament as a mystery. First Peter the first chapter states that Christ was chosen and destined from the foundation of the world, but was made public at that set time for our sake.

Some changes occur over time because people did not want to conform to the discipline or requirements of the old way. There are so many parents today that give their children more freedom than they were given when they were a child. Others changed because they felt like their parents had too many rules or were too strict. As a result, they made conscious decisions to give their children more freedom and less responsibility. Question, do you feel as if this represents you or do you know someone like this? Do you feel as if the children are better off because of the increase in freedom and decrease in responsibility? Other changes occur because more and more people are generally and blindly accepting alternative ways. Think about it. There are some who think that we should forget about using etymology to determine the meaning of a word. They believe that the meaning of a word depends not on its origin, but how it is being used or how the speakers of a language understand it. Hence, "bad" does not really mean bad depending on how you are using it. So then the "N-word" is a term of endearment depending who and how it is being said. Based on these standards people can exchange the truth of GOD for a lie and accept the lie as truth. How would we ever know the truth of GOD's word if we left it to our own personal interpretation (2Peter 1:20)?

Judges 2:8, 10-12 (KJV)
And Joshua the son of Nun, the servant of the LORD, died, being an hundred and ten years old..... Vs10 And also all that generation were gathered unto their fathers: and there arose another generation after them, which knew not the LORD, nor yet the works which he had done for Israel. Vs11 And the children of Israel did evil in the sight of the LORD, and served Baalim: Vs12 And they forsook the LORD God of their fathers, which brought them out of the land of Egypt, and followed other gods, of the gods of the people that were round about them, and bowed themselves unto them, and provoked the LORD to anger.

THE THREE-PART BEING

1Thessalonians 5:23
And the very GOD of peace sanctify you wholly, and I pray GOD your whole spirit and soul and body be preserved blameless unto the coming of our LORD JESUS CHRIST.

When GOD made man, He made him a being with three parts: spirit, soul (inner self) and body (outer appearance). The Apostle Paul prayed that GOD would completely sanctify (make holy, consecrate, and bless) us in every aspect of our being; our spirit, soul, and body. As we go through everyday life, we consistently see people trying to improve, enhance, or alter their physical, mental, and spiritual appearance or ability. When GOD made man, He first formed man's body/flesh out of the dust of the ground and then GOD blew into man's body the breath of life (the spirit of man). At that point, the Bible declares that man became a living soul. Thus, GOD performed the first cardiopulmonary resuscitation (CPR) by breathing His air (oxygen, the breath of life, or spirit) into the body and man came alive. The book of James chapter two says that the body without the spirit is dead the same as our faith without corresponding works is dead. The Bible declares that after GOD breathed into the nostrils of what He had formed; man became or began to exist. In this act of creation, GOD gives us a glimpse of how He functions in our faith. Everything that is alive in the mind of GOD may not appear to be living in the natural even though it seems to have taken shape. Even so, our faith causes things to exist in our minds even when it seems to be dead in the natural. If it appears to be dead that means that it has taken shape (everything is in place); however, there is no movement. That is because GOD has not breathed into it yet. For man, true life only begins after GOD breathes. For in GOD do we live, and move, and have our being (Acts 17:28).

Of all the creatures that GOD created, it was man that He (GOD) made in His image and after His likeness. Man is the only creature that GOD created in the natural in which He blessed and gave specific instructions to subdue and dominate everything else. And man is the only creature that after GOD formed it, He had to do something else to see it live, move, and have its being. Every creature that we see, GOD said, and it was; however, with man, GOD said, GOD formed, GOD breathed, and then man became. Not only did Adam's body come alive, but awareness of himself and his surroundings came alive as well. In the chapters to come, we will discuss the body and spirit and their effect on the way we think and live. We will then discuss the soul of man as well as its components in the chapters to come.

THE BODY OF MAN

The LORD GOD formed man's body (outer appearance) from the dust of the earth. In Genesis chapter two verse seven, the word for formed is a Hebrew word that essentially means to squeeze into shape, to mold into a form or to fashion. The word for dust is a Hebrew word that basically means powdered or gray dust, clay, ashes, mortar, or rubbish. In the book of Ephesians, the Word of GOD declares that we are the workmanship of GOD, created in Christ for good works. Similar to the potter and his lump of clay, are we in the hands of GOD (Genesis 2:7; Jeremiah 18:1-6). When Jeremiah was at the potter's house, he noticed the clay vessel that the potter was working on had been marred or blemished. Instead of discarding the clay, the potter began to apply pressure to refashion it into another vessel that pleased him. Because of disobedience (sin), man became marred or blemished in the hands of GOD; therefore, GOD refashioned another vessel again, as it pleased Him. Luke chapter three verse thirty-eight declares that Adam was the son of GOD. Due to Adam's disobedience, he became marred and ceased to look how GOD intended for him to look. Therefore, GOD refashioned Adam again. Thus, Jesus is the last Adam or the refashioned Adam.

For this reason it is written, the first man Adam was made a living soul; the last Adam was made a quickening spirit (1Corinthians 15:45). The Amplified version of Ephesians chapter two verse ten declares that we are GOD's handiwork, recreated in Christ Jesus, (born anew) that we may do those good works which GOD planned for us beforehand.

The potter can turn a lump of clay into a pot, but the pot will never become a pot of water until the potter decides to put water inside the pot. Whatever is placed on the inside of the pot is what gives it life or meaning; thus, our body would not come alive until GOD put our spirit and soul inside. "And the LORD GOD formed man of the dust of the ground, and breathed into his nostrils the breath of life; and man became a living soul" (Genesis 2:7 KJV). The lump of clay's sole purpose is determined by the will and desire of the potter. The lump of clay does not determine what it will become nor does it determine the path that it will take. The clay can only move by the power of the person carrying it or by what is placed on the inside to power it. After the potter takes the clay and makes an object for a specific purpose, he then gives it to someone else to use for their pleasure. Often times many cannot appreciate the thought and craftsmanship that is required to turn a lump of clay into a beautiful vessel. As a result, the vessel may be used for many purposes other than the purpose that was intended by its creator. Have you ever seen a cup that was supposed to be used for drinking; however, it is being as a spittoon or a urinal?

The book of Psalms one hundred thirty-nine verse fourteen declared that we are fearfully and wonderfully made. The works of GOD are marvelous, and our soul (inner self) should know this very well. Of all the creatures that GOD created, He took the time to form man with his own hands. GOD used the right amount of pressure to mold our lumps of clay into vessels to be used for His purpose. GOD said to Jeremiah before I formed you in your mother's womb, I knew you and designed you for a purpose (Jeremiah 1-5). Because GOD created us, He is the only one that can tell us who/what we are and what we are created for (our purpose). GOD wants us to live our lives according to His purpose, and yet we allow so many others to determine who we are and how we should be used. First Corinthians chapter six tells us that our body belongs to GOD, and yet He has given us the power to use as we see fit. The human body is so detailed, and yet many cannot see or do not want to believe and appreciate the fact that GOD took His time to mold our lump of clay into something wonderful. Just take a moment and ask yourself "am I living for GOD (my higher purpose) or am I only existing to be used by others?" I know that sometimes doing good things for others can make you feel used; however, if you are doing it for GOD, remember you were created for this, and you are fulfilling His purpose for your life. So really ask yourself, am I doing this for GOD or for myself or for someone else? If you are fulfilling GOD's purpose, don't get weary when doing good things for others because you will soon reap if you do not give up (Galatians 6:9).

Our human body is a type and shadow of the spiritual body of Christ. Our natural body is comprised of many members, and yet we have only one body. First Corinthians chapter twelve verse twelve states; that although the human body has many parts, it is still one body, and all the parts work together that they, being many, are jointly working as one: so also, is the body of Christ. Our body contains a number of cells that no man can accurately count (Revelation 7:9). These cells work in conjunction to form the different types of tissues and tissues work in cooperation to form the different organs, and then organs work together to form the various organ systems and ultimately the entire body. Each cell in the human body has a purpose as well as its own specific set of needs to survive or function at its optimal ability. Some cells work together to give us the ability to hear, and some cells work in conjunction to give us the ability to speak, but they are all a part of the same body. Each cell can send a signal that may affect other cells which in turn may affect tissue and then ultimately the entire body. And so GOD has created each of us as a type of spiritual cell with a specific function within the body of Christ. Some of us may be a part of the feet, and some may be a part of the hand, but we are all a part of the same body. As individuals (cells) within the body of Christ, we all have our specific purpose as well as our own individual needs to survive or function at our optimal ability. The same as the cells of the human body need the life-giving and the life-sustaining substance contained in our natural blood, so do we. As cells that are a part of Christ's spiritual body, we need the life-giving and life-sustaining substance that is found only in the blood of Jesus. If a natural cell goes without the appropriate blood supply for a prolonged period, it will begin to die, and if left unchecked, one dead cell can lead to the death of many other cells that are nearby. Deceased cells can release toxins that can ultimately affect the entire body. The same as with our natural cells, if we are not receiving the appropriate spiritual blood supply, and the nourishment that it brings we can begin to die and adversely affect others that are around us. Hebrews the twelfth chapter verse fifteen warns us not to allow any root of bitterness, resentment or hatred to be found growing in us because this can cause many others to be negatively impacted. Matthew eighteen verse eight declared that if your hand or your foot influences you or causes you to sin, cut it off and throw it away from you for it is better for you to enter into life crippled or maimed, rather than having two hands or two feet to be cast into everlasting fire. In this passage of scripture, GOD is not referring to our natural hands or feet but the individuals who make up the hands or the feet in the body of Christ. Verse seven of the gospel of Matthew chapter eighteen tells us it is necessary for temptations to come, but woe to the person that brings the temptation and causes other to sin and fall short of the glory of GOD.

Originally, our body was not designed to have input on what goes inside of it, nor was the body designed to affect what is put in it. Our body was designed to be a carrier for our soul (inner self/inner man) as well as provide awareness of the natural environment (natural awareness). Our body was designed to be a type of ark or container. The same way that

Moses placed the covenant, made of papyrus, into the ark (made of acacia wood), so is our spirit and soul placed into an ark made of clay. Think about it. The ark is called the Ark of the Covenant or Ark of the Testimony. This is because the ark was identified by what was on the inside and not by what it was made of. The Ark of the Covenant is a vessel that contained manna (the Word of GOD), and Aaron's rod that budded (GOD's chosen and GOD's life-giving Spirit), and the tables of the covenant (representing the laws and commandments of GOD). The LORD GOD told the Prophet Jeremiah that He would put His laws in the inward parts of man and write them in our hearts (Jeremiah 31:33-34). Hebrews chapter eight verse ten declares that GOD will imprint his laws in our minds, even upon our deepest thoughts, imagination and understanding. He will engrave them upon our hearts for a lasting record. The LORD also told Ezekiel that He would give us a new heart and put His Spirit within us, causing our spirits to be renewed. GOD said that He would remove our hardened and non-responsive (stony) heart from our body and replace it with a heart that is alive, sensitive and responsive to Him and His will (Ezekiel 36:26-27). The same as the Ark of the Covenant our body not only serves as a carrier for our inner man, but it also carries the Word of GOD, the Spirit of GOD and the laws/commandments of GOD. Our body was designed to carry what is on the inside and to be seen but not heard. GOD told Moses what to place inside the Ark of the Covenant. The ark had no say in the matter. Think about it, if we use a pot as a way to hold or carry water, the pot has no say in the matter, and it can only affect the water if it is dirty on the inside or by the limitations of its design. Being the creator that He is, GOD would not create us for a purpose that we cannot fulfill, and if there are limitations, He will give us what we need to overcome our limitations. We can do all things through Christ and His anointing that gives us strength.

Our biggest limitation is not the limitations of the body; however, it is the limitations of our thinking. If a pot is dirty, clean water can be used to wash away the dirt. Because of sin, our vessels have become filthy; even so, because GOD is so loving, gracious, and merciful He declared that He would sprinkle clean water on us, and we will be cleansed from all our filthiness (Ezekiel 36:25-27). GOD declared that He would cleanse and forgive us of all our sins (everything that makes us filthy), but we must confess our sins to Him and believe in Jesus Christ as our LORD and Savior. Jesus declared that we are cleansed through the words which He has spoken unto us (John 15:3). Ephesians chapter five verses twenty-five and twenty-six states that Christ loves us so much that He gave Himself up for us so that He might sanctify us, having cleansed us by the washing of water with the Word of GOD. As stated earlier, the body was not designed to affect or alter what is placed on the inside, and with every limitation, GOD has an answer. Remember the purpose of our natural body is to be a container and carry what GOD has put inside, not to have an effect or change it what's on the inside. Even if our body is placed in extreme conditions, this should not change our character. For example, if you place an empty pot on a stove and left it there the pot will become very hot; however, once you remove the pot from the heat and pour cool water into it, the pot automatically begins to cool down. The water is not heated or affected by the pot to the same degree that the pot is affected by the water. Although the pot (our body) may respond or feel the effects of the temperature changes immediately, the water (our soul) changes only when it is in the pot and is exposed to the heat for an extended period. Question, what are we trying to heat up? Is it, the pot or the water? GOD is not trying to see how our bodies will react to the heat. He wants to see how we (our inner self) will react to the heat. Everything that is built for the stove/oven cannot be placed in the microwave and vice versa. GOD knows which vessels are safe for the stove top, the oven, or the microwave. Some of us want GOD to do whatever He needs to do, but we want Him to do whatever it is quickly. Nevertheless, GOD says no because you were not built for that microwave experience. Some of us need high heat for extended periods of time for our inner man to be fully prepared. The question is what do we consider an extended period of time? In today's society, we all want everything to be quick or instantaneous. The Apostle Paul tells us that our afflictions are light and momentary when compared to eternity. James the fourth chapter verse fourteen tells us that our life is but a vapor, we are here for only a little while, and then we are gone. With all that being said, we all still want that microwave experience, and if we do not get instantaneous help, our character may begin to change. Is it that our character begins to change or is it that the heat is causing our true character to be exposed? Think about it, water is made up of two gases that when placed at the appropriate temperature or under the right pressure they bind together to form a liquid, but at its core, water is still two gases bound together. Remember the heat is not for the vessel; the heat is for what's inside. GOD does not want to save our body; He wants to save our soul. He is not trying to change our body, He is trying to change what's on the inside and sometimes the only way to see the change is by applying heat or pressure.

The response of the water, when placed under different conditions or pressures, determines the characteristics of the vessel. In other words, if the water is hot, then we say that it is a pot of hot water even if the pot itself is room temperature. Remember the ark was called the Ark of the Covenant because of what it carried and not because of what it was made of. Have you ever been to a restaurant and your server says to you "this plate is hot," but when you tasted your food, the food was cold? As stated earlier, the carrier was not designed to change the character of what it is carrying. Therefore, if you heat the plate without exposing the food to the same heat the characteristics of the food should not change. The environment may have an immediate effect on the pot/plate; yet, the characteristics of the objects inside the pot or on the plate should require a longer period of time in the environment to yield the same change. A hot stove may cause a pot to become hot immediately, but it should take a lot longer for the water to boil. Have you ever notice that hot water from the faucet looks different from the cold water. Prolonged and intense heat exposes the true gaseous nature of the water and as a result, the chemicals/minerals that were hidden in the liquid are now revealed in the gas.

Many times we cannot see these chemicals/minerals and the water looks and tastes normal to us. Another question is, what is normal? Often times we have accepted abnormal attitudes and circumstances as normal. Have you noticed things that were not accepted years ago are considered normal now? How about profanity in music or nudity on television (commercials and cartoons TV), years ago this would not have been accepted, but now it is accepted as normal. This should never be. GOD does not want us to be normal or typical, He wants us to be sanctified (set apart) and His standards have not and will not change. Ask yourself what else is today's society trying to push on you? What does society want you to accept as normal today that was not normal in the beginning? Just because it seems common does not mean that it should be accepted or treated as normal. GOD does not want ordinary for our lives He wants us to live extraordinarily.

I know that I have been talking about a pot or a plate, but I hope that you can understand the role that the body plays. Our body was designed by GOD to give us our natural shape and to carry what He has put inside (our soul and spirit), but it was not designed to define who we are and affect what we do. The soul or our inner self (inner man) has that responsibility. Our environment, circumstances, and mindset develop our character, and our spirit gives us life. In the fifth chapter of the book of Romans the Apostle Paul tells us that the sufferings [pressure, affliction, distress, persecution, harassment, discrimination, mistreatment, and tribulations (need I add anything else)] that we face in life may be used to develop patience. And if we utilize patience and endure the things that we suffer we will build strength of character and this strength of character will not allow us to lose hope. Our flesh or carnal man was not supposed to have a say on how we feel on the inside; it was only to make us aware of what was happening on the outside.

I have heard it said so many times, "fatigue will make cowards of men." Just because our body tells us that it is tired, does that mean we should quit? I was always told that a person will never know how far they can go until they push themselves to get there. Where is there? No one really knows. If I am tired and I stop running did my body make me stop or my mind? Now it becomes mind over matter. My inner man should tell me when it is time to stop when it realizes that my body has nothing left to give. We tell young athletes that there is a difference between being hurt and being injured. If an athlete is hurt, his body is sending a signal to his brain saying that there is pain present and we should stop; however, strength of character (inner will, drive) will say we can give more and it pushes through the light afflictions. If the same athlete is injured, his body will send a signal altering the brain that pain is present; however, in this situation, the inner man does an assessment and realizes that the body cannot go. There is a difference between not wanting to go any further and not being able to go any further; this should be determined by our inner man, not by our flesh. There will be several times in life when your body will tell you what you can or cannot do, but it is not up to your body. In the movie "Facing The Giants" the character Brock had a negative attitude and had written his team off, assuming they were going to lose their upcoming football game. The coach asked Brock to the death crawl blind-folded. The only requirement the coaching asked for was that Brock gives his very best. Throughout the scene, Brock was continuously saying that it hurts, and that he could not go any further, but his coach kept saying you can make it just give your very best. At the end of the scene, Brock made it one hundred yards with a 165-pound person on his back; when he initially thought, he could only make it to the fifty-yard line by himself. How many times have you said I cannot go any further; however, when you look back you have gone much farther then you thought you could. Our natural man sends limitations to our mind based on our environment, and if we are not careful, we will accept these limitations as exact truth. Our body was designed to tell us that it is cold; it was not designed to tell us that it is too cold. Because now the question becomes what is too cold and how did we make that determination? It is only too cold if you cannot deal with it and not because you do not want to deal with it. That is a decision for the inner man (state of mind) not the flesh. Years ago it was said that it was humanly impossible to run a mile in under four minutes and now the four-minute mark is the standard. Jesus tells us that the spirit is willing, but the flesh is weak (Matthew 26:41).

As stated before, our body (flesh) was designed to be a carrier of the human spirit and soul as well as give awareness of the natural environment. When GOD first made Adam, man's awareness of GOD and the heavenly or spiritual world was just as clear or evident to him as his awareness of himself and his natural surroundings. Adam's flesh was under control or subject to the will of his inner self. Man's flesh was seen but not heard. However, when sin entered into man, the body became a force to be reckoned with. The body gives us world consciousness or consciousness of our surroundings as well as a lust (desire and longing) for natural things. In Genesis the third chapter, we see several things occurring to demonstrate a greater awareness of the flesh and a loss of right relationship with GOD because of sin (disobedience).

First John chapter two admonishes us not to love the world, neither the things that are in the world. For all that is in the world is the lust of the flesh, the lust of the eyes, and the pride of life. These things are not of GOD but are of the world. In Genesis chapter three, Satan was able to deceive woman by using the lust of the flesh, the lust of the eyes, and the pride of life. These three areas are a direct result of our natural bodies and the desires thereof. If you read the Book of Matthew the fourth chapter verses one through ten (Luke 4:1-13), you find that Satan used the lust of the flesh, the lust of the eyes, and the pride of life to tempt Jesus. The Bible declares that Jesus was tempted in all points as we are, but he never sinned. After eating of the tree of the knowledge of good and evil both Adam and woman (for she was not called Eve until after the fall) realized that they were naked, so they sewed fig leaves together to cover themselves. This demonstrates a greater awareness of the flesh. Sewing the fig leaves together to cover their flesh is the first time Adam had done something and GOD had to make corrections. While Adam was naming all of the cattle, birds of the air, and beast of the field, GOD never went behind him to make changes to what Adam had already done. But when it came to the fig leaves being used to cover their nakedness, GOD was not pleased and had to make corrections even though Adam thought using the fig leaves was the right thing to do. Also, man replaced the reverence of GOD and the wiliness to commune with Him with fear and terror.

Many people are afraid to speak with the Father, and they do not believe that He desires to speak with them. When Adam realized that he was naked before GOD a fear came over him. This is the first time Adam ever felt afraid of being in the presence of GOD. So when GOD asked Adam where are you? Adam replied, "I was afraid because I was naked; so I hid" (Genesis 3:10). The Bible declares that Adam heard the voice of LORD GOD walking in the cool of the day. The phrase cool of the day represented a usual place or time that the LORD GOD met and communicated with Adam. Some think that this phrase represents early morning before the sun rises or evening when the sun is setting, and there is a cool breeze. According to Genesis three verse nineteen, Adam did not have to sweat to get the ground to produce for him until after he sinned. So before the fall (man's sin), it was always cool. The

Hebrew word for cool in Genesis the third chapter verse eight is the word "ruwach." This word is used to mean wind, breath, spirit as well as the mind. John the third chapter verse eight states that the wind blows where it will, and we hear the voice thereof, but we do not know where it comes from neither do we know where it goes; so is every one that is born of the Spirit. The wind represents the breath of GOD or the Spirit of GOD; therefore, Adam should not sweat in the presence of GOD.

In Ezekiel, the forty-fourth chapter verse eighteen the priest were commanded not to wear anything that would cause them to sweat when they ministering at the gates of the inner court or inside the temple. Saying all of this to say, when Adam heard the voice of GOD in the cool of the day, it was possibly dealing more with a spiritual atmosphere or climate caused by the presence of GOD rather than a specific time of day. Remember GOD made Adam in his image. The Hebrew word for image (tselem) is from an unused root that means to shade or a phantom. It is also used figuratively to mean an illusion, resemblance and hence a representative figure (especially an idol). Let's take a deeper look into the words "shade and phantom." The word shade can be defined as shelter from the heat and glare of sunlight or a place sheltered from the sun. Through the Scriptures we understand that GOD's glory shaded and overshadowed man; therefore, Adam lived in the shade or in the cool of the day. The Hebrew word "tselem" also means phantom. The word phantom can be defined as a disembodied spirit (ghost) or the similarity between a previously encountered person and one at hand. Jesus said, "if you have seen me then you have seen the Father." This is because there is a strong similarity between the person that Philip wanted to see and the person of Christ that Philip sees daily. GOD admonishes us not to make any images or idols to represent Him because He has already created us to be His representation. Why create an idol to represent GOD in the earth, when He has created us for that very purpose?

The boundaries of this world and the limitations of man's body have always been in place; however, Adam could operate with supernatural or spiritual power at all times. The Bible gives us a glimpse of the authority which Adam had before his fall. This is seen through the life of Jesus (the last Adam, 1 Corinthians 15:45). The laws of physics were intact with Jesus but this did not stop him from walking on water nor did the natural laws of this earth inhibit Christ from causing a fig tree to die from its roots just by speaking to it (Mark 11:14,21). We must understand that when GOD made man in his image and after his likeness he was not referring to the flesh or body (the carnality) of man. GOD formed man from the dust of the earth and crowned him with glory giving Adam the legal right to operate in the natural utilizing supernatural power. This GOD given ability allowed Adam to dominate here on the earth as He (GOD) is operating and dominating in the heavens.

As stated earlier the flesh is just a vessel designed by GOD to carry and give shape to the divine nature and presence of man which is the expressed image of GOD. The body of man was overshadowed or covered by the glory of GOD. The Bible declares that no flesh shall glory in the site of the LORD. In Genesis the third chapter verse six and seven it states the woman ate of the fruit and gave it to Adam also and he did eat. After they ate their eyes were opened, and they realized that they were naked; therefore, they sewed fig leaves together, and made aprons to cover themselves. We have to ask ourselves a question. Why are Adam and his wife just realizing that they are naked? What about all the other days that Adam walked and talked with GOD? The Bible states that they were both (Adam and his wife) naked and were not ashamed (Genesis 2:25). So what happened? When GOD breathed the breath of life into man, the nature of GOD filled man and the glory of GOD covered man and then man became a living creature in the image and likeness of GOD. The glory of the LORD overshadowed or shaded man, allowing GOD to see Himself when He saw man.

Revelation 19:8
And to her was granted that she should be arrayed in fine line, clean and white: for the fine linen is the righteousness of the saints.

The glory of GOD upon man or Adam appeared as an exceedingly white robe. This white robe represents the glory and righteousness of GOD that is given to man. According to the gospels of Matthew, Mark, and Luke, Jesus went on a mountain to pray, and he took with him Peter, James, and John. While Jesus prayed His appearance was altered, and his clothing became beyond white as snow. His clothing was so white it was obvious that no launderer on earth could have cleaned them. The Bible declares that Jesus was transfigured or transformed right before the eyes of the disciples because they saw Him covered with glory. The book of Zechariah the third chapter verses one through four, tells the story of Joshua the high priest standing before the angel of the LORD, and Satan standing at his right hand to resist (accuse or prosecute) him.

Revelation 12:10 (KJV)
And I heard a loud voice saying in heaven, Now is come salvation and strength, and the kingdom of our GOD, and the power of his CHRIST: for the accuser of our brethren is cast down, which accused them before our GOD day and night.

We must clearly understand that this incident is a spiritual encounter and not a natural encounter. In the natural Joshua was dressed in his priestly garments entering into the holiest of holies. However, in the spirit realm, Joshua was clothed with filthy garments as he stood before the angel of the LORD (you can look good and righteous in the natural but how do you look when you are standing in the presence of GOD and His angels). This actual account is given to illustrate unto mankind that without the LORD and his grace covering us, we stand before Him in filthy garments and our righteousness is as filthy rags (Isaiah 64:6). It is the LORD that causes our filthy garments to be taken away from us and our iniquity to pass from us. He will clothe us with a new outfit (a robe of righteousness). While reading this it necessary to point out that every natural action has a spiritual impact and everything that happens in the spirit will manifest in the natural. Adam's disobedience was a natural occurrence with spiritual implications. Our sins caused us to be separated from GOD, naked before GOD and caused the filthiness or unrighteousness of our flesh to be revealed.

2Corinthians 5:2-4 (KJV)
For in this we groan, earnestly desiring to be clothed upon with our house which is from heaven: Vs3 If so be that being clothed we shall not be found naked. Vs4 For we that are in this tabernacle do groan, being burdened: not for that we would be unclothed, but clothed upon, that mortality might be swallowed up of life.

Sin is like spilling spaghetti sauce on an extremely white shirt. No matter how small the stain it stands out to those that have eyes to see. Only GOD can cleanse our garments, but we have to allow Him to work in our lives. GOD wants us to live a holy life because He is holy. GOD wants us to present our bodies to Him as a living sacrifice (Romans 12:1). A sacrifice that is holy and righteous in His eyes, a life that He would accept. Do you remember Cain and how GOD did not accept his sacrifice (Genesis 4:3-6)? It is not enough to say that you have sacrificed for the LORD, but it must be a sacrifice that is acceptable unto Him as well. The level of sacrifice required is determined by the level of grace and mercy given. To whom much is given much is required. In Micah chapter six verse seven the question is asked, will the LORD our GOD be pleased with thousands of rams, rivers of oil, or even our firstborn in exchange for the sins of our souls? But the answer in verse eight tells us that all GOD requires of us is that we act justly, and love mercy (show and demonstrate His love) and to walk humbly with Him.

In first Peter, the first chapter verses fourteen through sixteen the Bible admonishes us not to conduct ourselves according to our previous ungodly cravings, desires or lusts that continuously lead us away from GOD. But to be as obedient children, conducting ourselves in a holy (sanctified, consecrated, righteous, and blessed) manner at all times. Our previous ungodly cravings stem directly from our carnal nature and are a direct result of the sinful nature that is inherited from Adam and his sin (disobedience). Verse nineteen of first Peter chapter one tells us that, Christ offered himself as a lamb without spot or blemish. The blemish of sin will always stand out in the eyes of GOD. GOD wants us to appear before his presence without spot. According to Ephesians five verse, twenty-seven Christ wants to present to himself a glorious church, a church without spot, wrinkle, or any such thing. Christ is coming back for a church that is holy and without blemish. Isaiah chapter fifty-nine verse two tells us that our sins have separated us from GOD that he will not hear, and he has turned his face. This is basically saying that the glory of GOD has departed from man, and without accepting Christ as our Messiah our flesh along with its carnal nature is no longer covered because of sin.

Samuel 4:21-22 (KJV)
And she named the child Ichabod, saying, The glory is departed from Israel: because the ark of God was taken, and because of her father in law and her husband. Vs22 And she said, The glory is departed from Israel: for the ark of God is taken.

The body (our outer appearance) is not sin itself. If GOD does not tempt us with sin, why would He give us a body that was the essence of sin itself? Our body is a gift from GOD, and it is the temple of the HOLY GHOST. Thus, we are required by GOD to take care of our bodies and glorify Him with it because our bodies belong to Him. For years people have understood the importance of physical exercise and its effect on our physical and mental health. However, this has not always been true in a lot of churches. There was a time when many Christians would focus solely on going to church and fellowshipping after church. As a result, their physical and mental health would go lacking. Thus, many would be excessively overweight, in poor mental and physical health; and as a consequence, mad with GOD because they were sick. Have you ever been participating in a worship service and everyone was celebrating the LORD through dancing and shouting? How long do you think it would last if everyone were physically out of shape? Their spirit would be willing to praise and celebrate GOD; however, the body would be weak and unable to continue. This weakness is not brought on by the devil but by our lack of exercise (taking care of your body because it is a gift from GOD).

1 Timothy 4:8 (NIV)
For physical training is of some value but godliness has value for all things,
holding promise for both the present life and the life to come. silver, or
stone, graven by art and man's device.

Every aspect of our being has a role to play in the praise and worship of our LORD. The Scriptures declare that we have been bought with a price. Therefore, we should glorify GOD with our body and our spirit because they belong to Him (1 Corinthians 6:20). Our body is not sin; however, the desires that are linked to our body or our flesh when left unchecked can cause us to disobey and stray from the will of GOD. For example, the desire for a man and a woman to come together intimately is of GOD. A part of GOD's original mandate to Adam as well as Noah was to be fruitful, multiply and replenish the earth. Therefore, Adam and his wife, Noah and his wife, as well as Noah's children and their wives had to get busy. The desire to have sexual intercourse is not the sin. But the desire for sex outside of how GOD commanded it to be is a sin. GOD intended for sex to be between a husband and his wife, male and female, a man and a woman in the covenant of marriage. Sex outside of this is a sin. That is why the Apostle Paul said that it is better to marry than to burn (because of sin – sex outside of marriage; 1Corinthians 7:9). The flesh or our carnal nature does not care about the rules of engagement that GOD has set in place; it just cares about the sex. It is up to the individual (our soul) to control this natural desire and make sure that he or she operates within the parameters of GOD. The Bible tells us that GOD formed our flesh out of the dust of the ground and when we die in this natural life our flesh (body) shall return to the dust (Genesis 2:7; Ecclesiastes 12:7). Consequently, when we make the statement, we must crucify or kill our flesh we are not literally talking about killing ourselves but rather deny the desires that originate from our flesh when they are in contradiction to the will and ways of GOD.

Our body gives us awareness of the world around us through our senses: hearing, sight, touch, taste, smell. Our body requires nutrients that come from various sources of food for energy. It does not care how you get the food it just wants the nutrients. The desires of our body if left unchecked are similar to that of an animal and can be more intense. For example, if an alligator or a lion has just eaten a sufficient meal, and another zebra walks past, the alligator or the lion will not move. Not so with humans, we will continue to kill regardless of what we currently have on hand. When our human nature is left unchecked, it will not tell us to stop until we have gone too far. In the wild, you will rarely see a lion that is obese, but in America over thirty-five percent of the population is obese. This says that our desire to eat food is greater than our need for food. Our carnal nature, when left unchecked, will cause us to become greedy or gluttonous which is a sin. This is why we are exhorted to bring our body, flesh, or our carnal desires under subjection (under control).

Using our natural senses our flesh sends impulses to our soul causing us to think or react based on the type and strength of the stimulus. The way our bodies move and respond to different stimuli is amazing. Scientists have discovered that when females are ovulating their bodies release pheromones causing them to give off an odor designed to entice (attract) the male species. The same is true of the male; their bodies produce pheromones that make them more attractive to the female. Have you ever noticed that some people appear more attractive or desirable during certain times of the month? What do you think when you see them or better yet why is that thought in your mind? There is a difference between being attracted to a beautiful person and having your flesh stirred on a deeper level. Most people do not realize that it is not just what we see that is stirring up our desire to mate, but it is also what we smell. Have you ever recently eaten a meal and shortly after someone comes along with some food that looks good and smells even better? How do you feel? Do you want to some? Do you taste it even though you were full a little while ago? Again, we must understand that our sense of sight and smell are sending impulses to our inner man. These impulses begin to affect how we think, reason and respond by stirring up our natural cravings. The more we watch them eat and the more we smell the food, the hungrier we get. Our natural needs that are motivated by our senses are often referred to as our animal (basic) instincts or our human (carnal, fleshly) nature.

Human nature can be defined as fundamental dispositions and behaviors of most individuals. The term carnal or fleshly nature represents our ways of thinking, feeling, acting, and reacting that are common to most humans or that are learned in social environments. The LORD admonishes us to forsake our ways and our thoughts; forsake our carnal nature and return to Him. His nature (ways of thinking, feeling, and acting) is higher than our nature (Isaiah 55: 7-9). GOD's desire is for us to no longer walk after the guidelines and standards of our fleshly nature, but rather submit to and follow after the leading of the Holy Spirit. The Bible declares that the Law of GOD was weakened by man's human nature because the awareness of our flesh with its carnal thoughts and purposes are antagonistic to the thoughts and purposes of God. From the beginning man's flesh along with its inherent nature was covered by the Spirit of GOD; however, Adam's disobedience resulted in the removal of GOD's covering, and man's flesh with its desires and impulses became a force to be reckoned with (Romans 8:1-8). The impulses from our flesh seek to cause us to respond/react knowingly or reflexively to external stimuli. We often hear individuals praying, asking GOD to forgive of sins that they have committed knowingly or unknowingly. To sin knowingly or consciously is to intentionally think, reason, and then respond to a stimulus based on knowledge or experience of what we have heard, seen, smelled, tasted, or touched. The strength of the stimulus or desire can cause an individual to deliberately do things that will put their lives, families, jobs, and so on in danger. To move reflexively is to react to a stimulus impulsively, automatically, or spontaneously based on stored information without conscious thought. A reflex is often an inborn (natural, instinctive, innate, inherited) response to an external stimulus that occurs and is acted upon without the stimulus reaching the level of mental alertness.

When individuals react reflexively or subconsciously, we often hear the phrase "it was an accident or I didn't mean too." Our carnal nature or instincts can cause us to react based on our five senses, and these senses will, in turn, affect how or what we think. If you think something may hurt, your body will tense up in response to a sensation of pain that has not occurred. You are getting a vaccination, so you brace yourself for the pain of the needle piercing into your flesh and while you are waiting; the pharmacist says ok have a nice day. You respond saying "is that it?" The pharmacist says "yes, that is it." Because of the image of the needle as well as possible past experiences your natural instinct was to become tense. Saying this another way; based on previous knowledge or sensual (visual) perception, you reacted reflexively and began to anticipate pain. In the book of Ezekiel chapter twenty verse seven, the LORD spoke to the children of Israel admonishing them to cast away every abomination and offensive thing that they indulged with their eyes while in Egypt. The LORD knew that the idols they saw with their eyes if not controlled and can become the images that they worshiped in their hearts. Our natural eyes are the entryway to our souls. The Bible declares that the light of the body is the eye and whatever our eyes become zoomed in and focused on can become the basis for us living our lives for GOD or living after the dictates of our flesh (Matthew 6:22-23). This is so true; some of the things that we desire most in life began with what we saw. Companies spend millions of dollars on marketing and advertising, trying to get us to see and hear about their products. Car companies, not only do they want us to see and hear, they want us touch and experience (come and test drive). If our natural senses become engaged, they can stir up cravings that appear ordinary and common; as a result, we begin to think, reason, and respond subconsciously or reflexively. Have you ever seen a car that you did not like the shape of initially? However, there are so many on the road, and you see it all the time. What happens to your feelings for the vehicle? The fact that you have seen the car everywhere creates the perception that the car is common, and if it is common than it must be okay. Over time, this process would lead to a point where you might say, "It does not look that bad" or "It's starting to grow on me." Now the car that you said, was ugly, and you would never buy, is the very car that you desire to purchase. What about the song that you did not like, and now you sing it all of the time? Why do you like the song now? Is it a good song or is it human nature?

Romans chapter seven verses twenty-three through twenty-five declares that our body parts have sensitive appetites and motivations that are controlled by a different rule of action. This law that is stimulating our flesh is in constant confrontation against the rules of our mind (our ability to reason). Because of our innate weakness, the inward desires of our inner man are constantly overruled by the strong cravings of our carnal man, and as a result, we become prisoners to our human nature or to the law of sin that dwells in the members of our body. Have you ever had a desire to change or do some things differently? However, when faced with a test or trial you made the same mistakes? How did you feel? Often times this makes us feel unhappy, deplorable, and worthless. For this reason, the Apostle Paul asked, O wretched man that I am, who can set me from the bondage of this body and its carnal desires? Thanks to God our inner man and its ability to think and reason can be strengthened as we grow in the knowledge Jesus Christ and accept Him as our Lord and Savior. With a renewed mind, we can ultimately choose to serve the Law of GOD even though our body wants to serve the law of sin.

1Peter 2:11 (AMPC)
Beloved, I implore you as aliens and strangers and exiles [in this world] to abstain from the sensual urges (the evil desires, the passions of the flesh, your lower nature) that wage war against the soul.

Our carnal nature also can be viewed as both a source of our norms or habits of behavior, as well as the basis of obstacles and limitations on life. Have you ever heard the sayings "no one is perfect" or "we're only human"? These suggest that our human or carnal nature is the source of inability to reach perfection or it is the fundamental flaw that inhibits us from living an extraordinary life. As stated earlier, GOD would not create us for a purpose that we could not fulfill, and if they are limitations, He will give us what we need to overcome them. We can do all things through Christ and His anointing that gives us strength. Our biggest limitation is not the limitations of the body; however, it is the limitations of our thinking. Our carnal nature consists of things that we are born with as well as things that are imprinted or inculcated on us early in our life. Because of Adam's disobedience sin entered and now we have a greater awareness or focus on carnal things; so much so that often times it is very difficult to control or satisfy our natural cravings once they are stimulated. We continuously want more of something even though we may not need more. The Bible declares that a person that loves money and prosperity will never be satisfied with the money they have because they will always want more (Ecclesiastes 5:10). Our fleshly desires can become like a wildfire consuming everything in its path when left uninhibited.

Romans 7:18 (AMP)
For I know that nothing good lives in me, that is, in my flesh [my human nature, my worldliness--my sinful capacity]. For the willingness [to do good] is present in me, but the doing of good is not.

The flesh of man does not denote sin but weakness and an inclination (proclivity, tendency, liking, or fondness) that can lead to sin. As Christians, we should believe that Jesus and GOD are one. For the Scriptures declare, in the beginning, was the Word, the Word was with GOD, the Word was GOD, and the Word came wrapped in flesh and dwelt among us (John 1:1,14-17). The Scriptures also declare that there are three bearing record in heaven, the Father, the Word, and the Holy Ghost and these three are one (1John 5:7). So then the question becomes if Jesus and GOD are one and GOD cannot be tempted with evil/sin according to James chapter one verse thirteen; how is it then that Jesus was tempted in all points as we are yet without sin? Hebrews chapter four verse fifteen says, for we do not have a high priest who is unable to understand our infirmities or our weaknesses, but we have one who has been tempted (tested, scrutinize, and examined) in every area or topic, just as we are yet he did not sin (he did not fall or fail any test).

Some would ask, how can Jesus be tempted with what we are tempted with now? Jesus was never tempted to with "meth" or "molly" or any other synthetic drug out today. However, I will ask you a question. Why do people use "meth" or "molly" or any other synthetic drug out today? It is not only about what you do; it is also about why you do it. If I can take away the "why," it becomes easier to stop doing the "what." In life, there are many subheadings and subtopics, but there are only three major heading or topics in which we are tested. Those areas are the lust of the flesh, the lust of the eyes, and the pride of life. James (the bother of Christ) asks the question, "From where do those fights and conflicts that are among you come from? Do you know their root cause?" He then gives them the answer, "They arise from your lusts (carnal and selfish desires) which are constantly at war in your bodies." The Apostle Peter admonishes us to abstain from fleshly lusts which war against our soul (1Peter 2:11).

The same way that woman (Eve) was tempted with the lust of the flesh, the lust of the eyes, and the pride of life, so was

Jesus and so are we. If our flesh or carnal nature in itself were a sin, then Jesus would not have been without sin. So we must understand that our flesh creates weakness, desires, cravings, or lusts that cause us to be baited or enticed and then drawn away from GOD's rules and His ways. And if we allow ourselves to be lured away from GOD to fulfill the desires of our flesh we are now in sin and on the path to destruction. The Spirit of Christ does not get hungry, but the flesh of Jesus does. Being hungry in the wilderness is not sin, but fulfilling that hunger by any means outside of GOD's set structure for food is a sin. The flesh of Jesus allowed him to experience what it is like to be hungry. The weakness associated with being in the flesh allowed Him to tempted and experience the struggle of accomplishing the will of GOD, knowing it will cost Him everything. Jesus said, "The spirit is willing, but the flesh is weak" (Matthew 26:41).

Our flesh or our natural body gives us the legal right to operate in the natural world. When we die in the natural our body is no longer alive, but our inner person is very much alive; therefore, death is a transition from the visible world to the invisible. The Bible declares that it is appointed unto a man to die once and after this comes the judgment. Depending upon our judgment there may be a second death, and this is the death of our soul (Hebrew 9:27; Revelation 21:8). Our inner being does not have a license to operate in the natural world without a physical body. However, we can be spiritually dead and still operate in the natural. The Apostle Paul writes in his letter to the Ephesians reminding them how they were once dead in trespasses and sins and how the Spirit of GOD has made them alive again (Ephesians 2:1-3). Paul was not writing this letter to a group of people that were physically dead but spiritually dead. We must understand that we can be alive in the natural and dead in spirit. The converse is also true. When we die the first death, if we are in CHRIST our earthly house (physical body) may dissolve but our soul is alive and well in GOD. The book of Ecclesiastes chapter twelve verse seven tells us that our flesh will return to the dust from which it was made, and our spirit will return to GOD who gave it to us. Only when we die in sin as an unbeliever is our soul forever separated from GOD. Remember, our righteousness is based on our faith. We are saved by grace as a result of our faith in Christ; and not because of any of our works that we use trying to establish our own righteousness. For whatsoever is not of faith is sin.

GOD created our bodies to be used as a vessel that allowed us to operate in the natural. He did not create flesh to be a hindrance to man's ability to function in the supernatural. Adam's disobedience caused our soul to be separated from GOD, and our body began a slow process of dying. The Father does not want us to die in a state where our inner man will be perpetually separated from Him, but He desires for us to live a life where we are eternally connected to Him. GOD looked for a man in the flesh that was worthy of being the sacrifice to save humanity. The Bible declares that GOD could not find anyone worthy to intervene and take responsibility for the sins of the world in his human body. GOD searched for a man that was willing and able to give his life as a ransom or an atoning sacrifice. As a type of kinsman-redeemer, he would justify many, making them righteous, upright before God, and in right standing with Him (Isaiah 59: 16-17; Isaiah 53: 10-12). The Scriptures declare that GOD looked and could not find anyone, so He came in the flesh and dwelt among us. Jesus came not only to show us the way but to be the way to everlasting life. If you confess with your mouth that Jesus is Lord and believe in your heart that GOD raised him from the dead, you shall be saved (Romans 8-10). The Father has made it just that simple for us. However, because sin is common, difficult, confusing and heartbreaking, it is a natural response to believe that there cannot be a simple answer that will fix all of the problems that are associated with sin. In our human nature, we love convenience and yet we are suspicious when the answers to life's problems seem too convenient or simple. Have you heard the saying "if it seems too good to be true, it probably isn't true"? Con artists and scammers use our carnal nature's desire for convenience and favor against us (e.g., a $30,000 car advertised as being sold for $10,000). It is amazing, even though we can sense within that something is wrong our human nature causes us to be attracted to it. As a result, we often experience disappointment and frustration because we have been taken advantage of. If this happens enough we can develop a mindset that inhibits us from believing in true miracles. The salvation that is offered to us through the gospel of Christ is too good, but it is true. GOD's plan of redemption may have been complex, but all we have to do to walk in his plan is very simple. However, due to the strongholds that we have developed in our minds, we ask "what's the catch?" The enemy exploits this stronghold by putting a false teacher in the church to perpetuate the feeling that someone is trying to get over. Have you heard someone say, the reason they do not go to church is that the preachers are crooks and all they are trying to do is get your money. Therefore, everything about GOD and His Christ must not be true. I have heard people say that used car salesmen are crooks and yet they still go to the lot and buy a used car. In actuality, many people are searching for an excuse not to believe the gospel of Christ. For some individuals, our fleshly struggles can be intense. Thus, living a sanctified life-style can be difficult and offering Christ as the answer seems too easy or convenient. In their minds, they are asking, what's the catch? Have you ever tried to teach someone a subject that they thought was confusing or difficult? No matter how basic you tried to make it; in their minds, they kept rejecting your teaching because a stronghold has been set up, that says complex problems require complex answers. They would say things like: "That can't be right." or "That seems too easy." It is amazing, you take something that seemed so difficult and gives them an easy solution, and they reject your answer not because it is wrong but because it is too easy. The Bible tells the story of Naaman, a mighty man of valor that was stricken with leprosy. Naaman came to the Prophet Elisha because he was told that Elisha could heal him. He came and stood at the door of Elisha expecting him to come out, but instead, Elisha sent his servant with a very simple message "go dip in the Jordan seven times, and you will be healed." Naaman was very angry and reasoned that the rivers where he came from were better than the Jordan River and if it was that simple he could have been healed a long time ago. One of Naaman's servants questioned him saying, if the prophet would have asked you a great or hard thing would you not have done it? So, why are you upset when he gives you an easy task (2 Kings 5: 9-13)? In Scripture, we see some of the most powerful miracles or acts of GOD happened after a simple prayer or simple action. The Apostle Paul told the church at Corinth, he feared that Satan might deceive them to the point that their minds would be corrupted, thus hindering them from receiving the simplicity of salvation that is found in the gospel of Christ (2 Corinthians 11:3). What makes the believer different from the non-believer that is struggling with the same sins? The answer is simple. You believe! You believe GOD is right and you are wrong; therefore, you repent and confess your sins to GOD. Walking in religiousness or self-righteousness does not make us different from those that would be called sinners. It is simply our faith in Christ and the belief that He gave His life as payment for our sins and GOD raised him from the dead. It is just that simple. We are no longer sinners because we believe in the gospel of Christ. As a believer, sin must no longer reside in our heart only in our flesh.

THE SPIRIT OF MAN

As we begin to talk about our spirit now is a good time pause for a moment. I want you to close your eyes and take three deep breathes (in your nose holding each breath for about three seconds and then slowly blow it out of your mouth). I want you to sit with your hands in your lap and with your eyes closed, I want you to focus on moving your toes. Next focus on moving your legs while you are moving your toes. Keep your eyes closed. Next focus on moving your fingers while you are moving legs and your toes. What did you sense or feel? There are a lot of moving parts. Does it seem chaotic? Let's try this again. Starting from the beginning with the deep breaths all the way through but this time I want you to continue to focus on your breathing (deep breaths) making sure to notice how the air fills your lungs causing your chest rise and fall. Do this for about three minutes. How do you feel? Does it seem as chaotic as before? When we focus on our breathing, it causes our mind to slow down creating a rhythm or harmony between our breathing, mind, and body. Everything appears to become less hectic. The Greek word for spirit is the word pneuma. Pneuma is also defined as wind or breath. Amazingly, when we focus on the things of the spirit or our breathing everything else has to calm down and get in synchronization. This is how it was from the beginning. When Adam was created, he had very little awareness of his flesh. He was naked and not ashamed. He operated as a spirit being with a soul, living in a body. After his disobedience, he began to operate as a fleshly being that has a soul and spirit.

The spirit of man is the part of our being that is most like GOD. When we confess with our mouth that Jesus Christ is Lord and believe in our hearts that GOD has raised him from the dead, the Spirit of GOD takes up residence and dwells in us. The Bible declares that GOD is a Spirit and those worshipping Him must worship Him in spirit as well as in truth. The Bible also declares that GOD desires and seeks for those that will worship Him in spirit and in truth (John 4:23-24). GOD uses our spirit to communicate with us. GOD desires to communicate with us Spirit to spirit. Romans chapter eight verse sixteen tells us that the Holy Spirit itself joins with our spirit supporting and testifying to the fact that we are no longer slaves to sin but rather the children of GOD. The Apostle Paul declared that our natural eyes have not seen, nor have we heard with our natural ears nor has it entered into our hearts, the things which GOD has prepared for those that love Him. But GOD has revealed them unto us by His Spirit. The things of GOD no one knows, except the Spirit of GOD and GOD has given us His Spirit that we might know the things that He has freely given unto us (1Corinthians 2:9-14). GOD can hear and understand the carnally minded; however, the carnal minded can not necessarily hear or understand GOD. Please understand this does not mean that GOD does not speak to carnally minded people, but rather it is hard for them to hear GOD or believe GOD when he does speak. When we are carnally minded, GOD uses other forms of communication to speak to us. Often times GOD will give us a sensing, a knowing, or intuition that comes from Him through our spirit and becomes a thought in our mind. In the twentieth chapter of the Exodus, GOD spoke audibly to the people without filtering His voice, and the people became afraid. They said unto Moses "You speak with us, and we will hear; however, do not allow GOD to speak because we are afraid that we may die." Also, we see in other passages that when GOD spoke some only heard the sound of thunder and they were not able to discern the voice of GOD. Therefore, in most cases when GOD speaks to us his voice, choice of words, etc. is filtered through our spirit, and it becomes evident in our mind as a thought or in a language that we can understand and, in a voice, that we can accept. When GOD spoke to the Prophet Samuel for the first time, GOD's voice sounded like Eli's voice (1Samuel 3:1-10). GOD spoke to Samuel in a voice that he could understand and would not be afraid of. The same is true in Acts chapter two; GOD used his apostles to speak to the multitudes. The multitudes outside were perplexed and began to ask "how is it that we hear them in our own language isn't everyone who is speaking a Galilean?" The Bible declares that those who were inside began to speak in different or foreign languages (diverse tongues) as the Spirit gave them utterance. GOD speaks to us in many different ways (dreams, visions, nature, etc.); however, the method by which GOD desires to use when speaking to his people is Spirit to spirit. We must remember that GOD made us in His image and in His likeness; thus, He created us to be spirit beings that live in a body and possess a soul. The Bible declares that our body is the temple of the Holy Ghost, and the Spirit of GOD dwells in us. Our spirit is the holiest of holies in this temple, and it is the place where the Spirit of GOD resides. When we give our lives to Christ, our faith allows His Spirit to bond with our spirit, so tightly, causing us to become one (1 Corinthians 6:17-20).

1 John 4:15
Whosoever shall confess that JESUS is the Son of GOD, GOD dwelleth in him, and he in GOD.

Just as our flesh or body gives us consciousness of our natural/physical surroundings, our spirit gives us an awareness of our spiritual surroundings. The same as in the natural, we see, hear, smell, taste, and touch spiritual things because of our spirit. The Book of Psalms chapter thirty-four verse eight tells us to taste and see that the LORD is good. In the Book of Acts the twenty-second chapter, the Apostle Paul declared those that were with him definitely saw a light, and were afraid; however, they did not hear the voice of Jesus. By the power of the Spirit, the Prophet Elisha was able to see the chariot of Israel and the horsemen thereof, while others only saw a whirlwind (2 Kings 2:11-12). The Prophet Elisha's servant woke up one morning and saw an army surrounding him and Elisha. He was very afraid because of what he saw with his natural eyes, but the Prophet prayed that GOD would open his servant's eyes that he might see in the spirit. The Prophet understood that his servant was not looking in the spirit realm because he was spiritually blind (2 Kings 6:14-17). The Bible declares that we have eyes to see yet we do not see anything and we have ears to hear, but we cannot hear because of our rebellion against GOD (Ezekiel 12:2). However, when we are in the right relationship (justified) with GOD, our spiritual senses come alive, and through use, they are sharpened. When our inner man is influenced solely by our human nature, it becomes difficult to see, hear, or understand the things of GOD since they are spiritually discerned and we are considered to be spiritually dead.

As stated early, Ephesians chapter two verse one tells that we were once dead as a result of our sins and transgressions; however, we are now made alive by the power of the Spirit of GOD. In this passage of scripture, the Apostle Paul did not write a letter to a group of people that were physically dead but a group that was considered spiritually dead. The Spirit of GOD is our source of life; He is like the air that we breathe. He is the root, and we are the branches and separated from him we cannot survive. If someone receives a bouquet of long stem roses, are the flowers still alive? The roses bloom, and they still have their fragrance but are they alive? Separated from the root, the roses are not living; they are going through the motions of life but they surely going to die. There is life in the stem but that life is fading and no matter how much water you put them in they are still going to die. Our life without the spirit is like a rose without its roots; we are going through the motions of life, but we are surely going to die. Our spirit without the Spirit of GOD is like a person on death row; a dead man walking, the switch has not been pulled, but it's just a matter of time. With all that being said, I am amazed at how someone with what we call a green thumb can take a leaf or a stem from a dying plant and cause it to live. I am so glad GOD knows how to resuscitate us and cause us to live again. Therefore, it is written, the first Adam became a living soul (an individual personality); while the last Adam (Christ) became a life-giving Spirit, restoring the dead to life (1 Corinthians 15:45 AMPC).

Before we became spiritually alive in GOD, there were certain actions (immoral – i.e., fornication, lying, etc.) we did that had no effect on how we mentally or emotionally felt. However, once our spirit man came alive, we developed a consciousness of GOD, and those same things caused us to feel awful on the inside. The Apostle Paul reveals that we must compare spiritual things with spiritual because our natural man cannot understand or receive the things of GOD. To our carnal mind, things that are revealed by the Spirit of GOD appear to be foolishness and unbelievable or just unspiritual. Paul told the church at Corinth that he could not talk to them as if they were spiritual men, but as to non-spiritual men in which the carnal nature was dominating. Paul stated that they were unspiritual, living and behaving according to the nature of the flesh, acting like mere unchanged men.

The Apostle Paul also stated that he had to feed them with milk and not with meat because they were too immature spiritually to handle spiritual meat (1 Corinthians 3:1-3). Hebrews the fifth chapter verses twelve through fourteen states, everyone who only uses (lives off) milk for their spiritual nourishment is a person that is unskilled in the elementary principles of the Word of God because in the spirit realm they are still a baby. Solid food is for those who are spiritually mature in Christ. First Peter chapter two verse two tell us that as newborn babes, we should desire the genuine, unadulterated spiritual milk of the Word, that by it we may grow. But can you imagine a five-year-old that has been fed nothing but milk? They will not have the strength to stand up let alone walk. Milk is good in the early stages of life because it helps in the development and formation of strong bones that provide structure to the body. It also has proteins that are helpful in the production and strengthening of young and immature muscles; however, as we grow, milk alone does not provide the body with all of the proteins and nutrients necessary to produce healthy (strong and mature) muscles.

The same way that we appreciate how vital it is for us to feed our natural bodies and to grow in the knowledge and understanding of natural laws; it is even more important that we feed our spirit man and grow in the knowledge and understanding of the Word of GOD and His spiritual laws and principles. Therefore, we must study the Word of GOD and pray (with the spirit and with an understanding) so that we may grow and mature spiritually. It is not enough just to read the Word; we must be a student and study the Word. The Scriptures declare that the way in which our mouth (tongue/palate) tastes natural food so does our ear tests words (Job 12:11; Job 34:3). Also, the Bible tells us the same measure of thought and study we give to the Word of GOD that we hear will determine the measure of virtue (moral excellence and power coming from GOD) and knowledge that we obtain (Mark 4:24 AMP). This is similar to a sheep chewing his cud. Cud is partially digested food that is regurgitated to be rechewed and swallowed. This is done to extract more nutrients from the grass or feed that was originally swallowed. Just because we read a Bible verse does not mean that we have received all of the revelation that GOD has intended for us to receive. We must learn to swallow (understand and accept) the Word of GOD and then bring it back up so that we can chew on (study) it some more, allowing GOD to release greater revelation. As we feed the Word of GOD to our spirit man, his influence on our soul increases, our faith grows, and as a result, we have greater access to the grace of GOD. According to Paul's epistle to the Romans, by faith, we have access to the grace of GOD in which we stand. Thus, when we grow spiritually our impact on the spiritual as well as the natural environment begin to shift or increase. We begin to walk in a greater sense of dominion.

One of the ways we can build up our spirit man is by praying in our heavenly language (praying in tongues). Although speaking in an unknown tongue is a source of controversy, I feel that it is very important for us to discuss its purpose and value to the believer. The Bible declares in first Corinthians the fourteenth chapter that any believer that speaks in an unknown tongue does not speak to man but unto GOD. The Scripture goes on to say that when a believer is speaking in an unknown tongue, his spirit is praying or communicating, but his natural mind does not appreciate anything that is being said. Although no man understands what is being said, the mysteries of GOD are being declared by the inspiration and empowerment of the Holy Ghost. By the power and unction of the Holy Spirit, our spirit has the ability to express itself with sounds and groaning, things that cannot be uttered or articulated in an understandable language. In other words, we begin to speak in an unknown tongue. Even though the carnal mind cannot receive nor understand the things of GOD, we must remember that the same Spirit that searches the hearts of men and knows what is in the mind of the GOD is this same Spirit that dwells in us. First Corinthians chapter two verse twelve tells us that GOD has given us the Holy Spirit that we may be able to realize, grasp, and appreciate the things that He is so freely and abundantly giving to and bestowing upon us. Our reborn spirit is in constant communication with the SPIRIT of GOD, and as a result, it has a greater understanding and awareness for the things that GOD has prepared for us.

Therefore, when we pray in an unknown tongue, we are able to pray and communicate back to GOD the things that He has already promised to us. This type of prayer is very powerful. The same way that prophecy can edify the church as well as be used as a weapon in spiritual warfare; so, can speaking in an unknown tongue be a weapon to the individual that is speaking. The book of Jude admonishes us to pray in the HOLY GHOST to build ourselves up. Using our most holy faith as the foundation, praying in tongues helps us to continuously make progress, building up our spiritual self, like a building starting from its foundation continues to rise higher and higher as it is built upon. Often times in stressful situations we realize that one of our weaknesses is our inability to know how to pray as we ought, let alone knowing what to pray for. Have you ever been in a situation that was extremely stressful? Have you ever felt overwhelmed by the pressures of life? I have been there on several occasions. I can remember how difficult it became to pray or read the Word of GOD. You wake up in the morning, and the last thing you would think about doing is saying a prayer. Where to start? What to say? You try to pray with an understanding but you find yourself silently thinking about your problems. You find that you are no longer praying but rather rehearsing life's situation and circumstances in your head. How strong do you feel? Thanks be to GOD because He has given us His Spirit to help us with this infirmity (weakness). The Holy Spirit uses our spirit, praying through us, making intercession to GOD on our behalf (Romans 8:26). Jesus sits at the right hand of the Father making intercession for us and the Spirit of GOD dwells in us making intercession to GOD through us.

Speaking in an unknown tongue may be initiated by the power of the HOLY GHOST, or it may be initiated by the individual as an act of his/her own will. I am not saying that someone can teach you how to speak in tongues but rather once this ability is activated you can turn it on or off at your discretion. According to first Corinthians chapter fourteen, the Apostle Paul declared that he would, as an act of his free will, pray with his spirit as well as with an understanding. Speaking in an unknown tongue edifies or strengthens our spirit, but it does not help our understanding or others unless there is an interpretation. Praying with both is very important to each of us as believers. Our natural man has a need to hear what it deems important being expressed to GOD in prayer. What we think we need may not be the most important thing in the grand scheme of GOD's plan but none the less we still have an unconscious desire to hear our needs expressed in a way that we can understand and appreciate. It is also a subconscious issue of trust and control. Can you imagine having someone speaking on your behalf and you cannot understand anything that is being said? How secure would you feel? Do trust in everything that is being said on your behalf? Have you experienced a situation where you walked into an elevator, and two people were speaking in English but the moment you got in they began to speak in another language? What goes through your mind? Are they talking about me? I would sometimes jokingly say "What did you say about my momma?" When we do not understand we do not have a sense of control. If I always have to trust you, that means that you are always in control. We are built to have dominion and have a sense of control. This is why it is important to pray with an understanding as well as with the spirit. Praying in an unknown tongue is important because there are several times when we are not in a mental place in order to pray for ourselves let alone pray for others; however, when we pray in an unknown tongue our spirit is praying the will of GOD for our life even when we do not understand what is being said. We must build ourselves up in our most holy faith by praying with our spirit by the power of the Holy Ghost (Jude 1:20). Building up our spirit empowers us to see and perceive, as well as hear and understand what the Spirit of Lord is saying to His church and us.

THE SOUL OF MAN

In the tabernacle of Moses, there was an outer court, inner court (holy place) and the holiest of holies. The outer court is the place where sacrifices were made, on the brazen altar. The outer court also contained the brazen laver, which is the place where the priest would look in the mirror so to say and wash before entering into the inner court or the holy place. The outer court is a place of repentance; it is the place where we humble ourselves and crucify or put to death the deeds of our flesh as we move from sin consciousness to self-awareness. The Word of GOD tells us to present our bodies as a living sacrifice; by the power of the Holy Spirit, we do mortify the deeds of our carnal nature. As we progress, we find ourselves in the inner court. The inner court contained a table for showbread, a lamp stand, and the altar of incense. The holiest of Holies contained the Ark of the Covenant, and it was the place where GOD would speak to the high priest. The outer court represents our body; the inner court represents our soul, and the holiest of Holies represents our spirit. We have briefly talked about the body and spirit, now it is time to talk about the soul of man.

THE SOUL OF MAN

Mark 8:36-37
For what shall it profit a man, if he shall gain the whole world, and lose his own soul? Vs37 - Or what shall a man give in exchange for his soul?

According to the Strong's Concordance, the Hebrew word for soul is nephesh, and it refers to the essence of life, a breathing creature, appetite, body, breath, heart, lust, man, mind, mortal person, and pleasure. The Greek word for soul is the word psuche which corresponds respectively to the Hebrew word nephesh and it also refers to heart, life, mind, and soul. In addition, the Greek word psuche parallels our English word psyche which is by one definition the soul, mind, or personality of a person or group. When GOD formed man out of the dust of the earth, He only formed the outer appearance of man. The same as the potter, GOD, used the clay of the ground to form the vessel that would carry the life of man. Remember, the potter can turn a lump of clay into a pot but the pot will never become a pot of water until the potter puts water on the inside. Whatever, is on the inside of the pot gives it life or meaning; thus, our body would not come alive until GOD put our soul and spirit inside. The body of man had no life or character until GOD breathed into his nostrils the breath of life and only then did man come alive (Genesis 2:7). The same as a caterpillar is transformed into a butterfly or moth so did the body of man become a living soul. The Word of GOD declares that GOD breathed into his nostrils and man became a living soul. The word became is the past tense of become and it means to come into existence or to undergo change or development. Thus, GOD's focus was no longer on the body (caterpillar) or what man was. The LORD's attention was now on what man had become, a living soul (the butterfly). Leviticus chapter seventeen verse eleven states that the life of the flesh is in the blood. In the same way that the LORD gave Adam the green plants for food, the LORD declared that every living creature will be food for Noah and his sons. The only stipulation was that they could not eat the meat of an animal while its blood or its life was still in it (Genesis 9:3-4). The Bible stated in Genesis chapter thirty-five that the soul of Rachel was departing, and as a result, she died. The Scriptures also tells us about a situation where a child had died and the prophet Elijah prayed to the LORD asking for the soul of the child to return to him again. The LORD heard Elijah's prayer and allowed the soul of the child to come into him once more, and the child regained consciousness (1Kings 17:21-22). These scriptures are used to help us realize that the soul represents the life and consciousness of man. Therefore, a person that is devoid of their soul is truly dead. Most times, when we hear of someone not having a soul or heart; we are often times referring to a person that lacks compassion or a person whose actions are so dark or evil that they seem to go against human nature. This individual is not considered physically dead, but their inner man is in a place of sin and it is heading down the path to eternal damnation and the death of their soul.

In the same way that the LORD uses three tenses or dimensions to describe Himself, the temple, man, and even salvation. When we are discussing being dead or death in the scriptures there is a difference. We must understand that there are three categories or forms of being dead. There is physical death, spiritual death, and the death of our soul. The word dead means to be destitute of life. It means lacking animation or lacking the power to move, feel, or respond. The word dead also is used to describe something that is no longer producing or functioning. With this in mind, we should understand that we can be physically alive and yet spiritually dead. Our flesh is alive; however, our spirit is separated from GOD, and as a result, it is deprived of life and lacking power.

Ephesians chapter two verse five declares that we were spiritually dead as a result of our sins, but GOD has jump-started or quickened our spirit making us spiritually alive together with Christ. We can experience physical death due to our human spirit leaving our body. Our mortal body is in the grave and lacking animation or the power to move, feel, and respond. In this state, our body returns to the dust from which it was made, and our spirit returns to GOD who gave it to us (Ecclesiastes 12:7); however, the location of our soul depends on our relationship with Christ Jesus. Finally, we can experience the death or destruction of our soul. If our soul gives us self awareness; what happens to us if it is destroyed? If our soul is dead, we are deprived of life or lacking animation in our mind, will, and emotions. If our soul or inner man is no longer functioning, we are truly dead (dead, dead).

Ezekiel 18:4
Behold, all souls are mine; as the soul of the father, so also the soul of the son is mine: the soul that sinneth, it shall die.

The term dead may be used as an adjective or descriptive word. It is also used as a noun when describing a group or individual that is deceased (i.e., the dead in Christ). However, when we look at the term death in the book of Revelation, the word death appears to be used as a noun (a person, place, or thing). I looked, and behold a pale horse, and the name of his rider was Death, and Hell followed closely behind him. They both were given authority and power on the earth, to kill with sword, with hunger, with death, and with the beasts the earth (Revelation 6:8). In the book of Revelation, Christ declared that he has the keys of hell and of death; as if death was a place that could be locked and unlocked (Revelation 1:18). Also, the Word of GOD declares that death and hell will give up the dead that are in them, and they both will be cast into the lake of fire (Revelation 20: 23-14). In these passages of Scripture, we clearly see the word death is used as a person, place or thing. This is important to understand as it relates to our soul because there are two distinctly different deaths that we may face. The first death is the result of our soul departing from our natural body; thus our flesh is lacking power or animation. Unless Christ returns before we die, the first death is a mandatory scheduled appointment. As it is appointed unto men once to die, but after this is the judgment (Hebrews 9:27). In the book of Revelations chapters two, twenty, and twenty-one, we find statements concerning the second death. The second has nothing to do with the death or decay of our flesh, but it is the destruction of our soul in the lake of fire. The gospel of Matthew chapter ten admonishes us not to be afraid of anyone who may be able to kill our body, but they have no power to destroy our soul. Jesus tells us, rather to fear GOD because He is the only one who has the power to kill our body and destroy our soul. Remember, in the book of Revelation the word death appear to be a person, place, or thing. Therefore, the person or thing called death can be cast, or thrown into a place or thing called death. It can also participate in the second death. In Scripture, we clearly see there was a first and second Adam and the first Adam was nothing to be compared to the greatness of the second Adam. In the same line, we understand that there is a first and second death; however, the first death is nothing to be compared to the second death. The second is greater and more terrifying in every aspect than the first. The Scriptures declare that the person who overcomes the world by a continued and unwavering faith in Jesus Christ or anyone who takes part in the first resurrection, cannot be hurt by the second death because it has no power over them (Revelation 2:11 and Revelation 20:6). However, the fearful, unbelieving, those that are lacking moral character, murderers, sorcerers, idolaters, anyone who practices or teaches false religions and such like will not escape the eternal judgment that leads to the second death. The Word of GOD declares that even liars, those who knowingly deceive and twist the truth, will have their part in the lake of fire, which is the second death. As a believer and follower of Christ, we should not be afraid of this statement because we trust that Jesus died for our sins. For the wages of sin is death, but the gift of GOD is eternal life through the finished works of Christ Jesus (Romans 6:23). This first resurrection includes those who participated in what we call the rapture (1Thessalonians

4:13-18) as well as the resurrected Christian martyrs who have given their lives during the tribulation period (Revelation 20:4). Remember, it is a war for our soul. It is about our eternal soul salvation. Although our flesh may try to influence what we say or do, it is the soul of man who makes the decisions. The decay or our mortal bodies may limit our time on this earth; however, it does not determine our eternal destination or duration. It is the inner man who controls how we think, feel, and act. Therefore, the LORD receives our spirit, changes our bodies, and judges our soul.

Malachi 3:3
And he shall sit as a refiner and purifier of silver: and he shall purify the sons of Levi, and purge them as gold and silver, that they may offer unto the LORD an offering in righteousness.

The Word of GOD teaches us that our body is the temple of the Holy Ghost. The same way that items in the Tabernacle of Moses had to be in perfect alignment; our mortal body and our soul must come into alignment with our spirit. Remember, when we are joined to the LORD, His Spirit joins with our spirit, and we become one with Him. In the same way that we must learn to control our flesh, we also must learn to discipline our mind, our will and our emotions bringing them under the influence of the Holy Spirit. We must develop unity between our spirit, soul, and body. The LORD GOD asked, how can two walk together if they are not in agreement with each other (Amos 3:3) It is truly difficult to move forward, let alone walk a straight and narrow path if individuals on the same team are pulling in different directions. We must develop unity and agreement not only with our spirit, soul, and body; we must also develop a unity or oneness within our soul. The Bible declares, a man that is wavering between two opinions is double-minded, and as a result, he is unstable in all of his ways. If the components that make our inner man are out of sync and pulling us in different directions, instability will be created within our soul (James 1:6-8). Throughout the Bible, we can see the importance of unity and the power and glory that unity results in or releases. There is great power when a group of individuals work together as one.

In this same way, there is a great awaking and creation of inner strength when our mind, will, and emotions are all working in conjunction to accomplish a common goal. Matthew chapter six verse twenty-two tells us that the light of the body is the eye and if our eyes are single or focused on the same thing, then our entire body will be full of light. I can remember when I was in the Marine Corps, my unit was using the M60 A1 tanks. These tanks had what we called frog eyes on both sides of the turret. The frog eyes were a part of the rangefinder system in the tank. I believe they are a perfect example of the necessity for the eyes to be single. In the M60 Tank, when we are trying to find the range of a target, we must make sure that both eyes are clearly focused on the same target. Thus, they are providing one clear picture. If there is double vision, we will not hit our target. Oneness or singleness of our mind, will, and emotions is so important to us hitting the mark that GOD has set for us through Christ.

In Psalms one hundred three, we discover something amazing, and it can be a powerful tool to help us stay focused during times of adversity. In this passage of scripture, we find King David commanding his soul to bless and lovingly praise the LORD. The King then commands his soul and all that is deep within him to bless the holy name of the LORD. David understands it is his soul that is the seat of his existence, and it is with his soul that he blesses, curses, hopes, trusts, and remembers (Psalms 103:1-6). This is why the Bible declares that we must love the LORD our GOD with the entirety of our inner being. The LORD requires that we love Him with our thoughts, feelings, imaginations, mental faculties, abilities, might, and power. That is to say, love the LORD our GOD with the life force which animates our body and gives us our very existence. If we continue to look at Psalms one hundred three, we find David reminding his soul that when it was in sin and GOD forgave him. The King also brings his inner man in remembrance of the fact that it was sick and the LORD healed him. He reminds his soul that it was in a pit of bondage, and the LORD GOD redeemed him. Not only that but the LORD also crowned his soul with loving kindness and satisfied the years of his life with good things; renewing his inner strength like that of an eagle. The psalm writer then asks himself a question. He asks, "Why are you depressed and discouraged my soul? Why are you crying and so tumultuous within me?" It is as if he is saying, "Get a hold of yourself and get in line." He is commanding his inner man to hope and trust in GOD. The psalm writer summons his will and says, "I will yet praise the LORD because He is the comfort and strength of my countenance, He is my GOD" (Psalms 42:5, 11). Through self-talk, he is commanding and disciplining his soul to maintain faith in GOD. He is telling his emotions, "It is not about how I am feeling at this current moment. It is about my will and what I decide to do." This is what we must tell ourselves during difficult times in life. We must command our inner man to get up, straighten up, wake up, and if necessary shut up. Have you ever had to make yourself do something that emotionally you did not want to do? Have you ever felt like quitting, but you said to yourself, "I cannot stop now"? There times when we are thinking about something that will lead us down the wrong path. It is at that time we must talk to our inner man; whether, it is our mind, our will, or our emotions we must bring them into alignment with each other and ultimately with the Word of GOD.

Our soul gives us life, expression, consciousness and an awareness of our inner being. Consciousness may be defined as a state of being, that is characterized by sensation, emotion, volition (will, desire, or choice) and thought. Consciousness also is considered a heightened level of psychological (mental and emotional) awareness. By reading the Holy Bible, you would get a sense that our mental and emotional state is very important to GOD. Remember, the Father wants to change us into another person by changing the way we think. It has been said, if we change the way we think, we can change the way we live. So many people spend their lives trying to find happiness and achieve success, not realizing that the journey to true happiness and success begins with a focus on themselves and not their circumstances. It is not about getting out of Egypt (bondage). It is about getting the oppressive mindset out of us. John, the Apostles, declared that his desire was for us to flourish in every way, to be successful in business affairs, and to be in good physical and mental health as our soul flourishes in every way. If our inner man is growing in a healthy manner, our body, mind, and business will follow. However, if our soul is not growing appropriately, our point of view will become shaded and our idea of what is true success and happiness will seem as fleeting ideas. This lack of development in our soul or inner man means that we are not operating in a state of complete psychological well-being. We are suffering from an illness. The word illness in old times was used to mean wickedness; however, now it is used to identify a condition of being unhealthy in your body or mind. It is a specific condition that prevents your body or mind from working how it was designed at an optimal level. Based on the processes that make up our soul; soul sickness would refer to alterations in a person's thinking, emotion or behaviors that create distress and lead to impaired functioning.

Psalms 41:4 (KJV)
I said, LORD, be merciful unto me: heal my soul; for I have sinned against thee.

Question, what if an individual's thinking, emotions, and behaviors are consistent with a larger group, is the individual still considered ill? What if a person is functioning in a way that is deemed necessary for survival in their environment;

will their behaviors be considered to be impaired? Have you ever talked to someone who was doing something that you felt was extreme behavior? You might ask why? You may say that's crazy. However, their response would be "everyone is doing it." Why are you using drugs? Everyone is doing it. Why are you hooking up with random people and having unprotected sex? Everyone is doing it. The fact that in their minds, everyone is doing it, makes their thinking, emotions, and behaviors appear normal to them, and as a result, it does not create a feeling of distress or impaired functioning within. Thus, by definition, they are not feeling sick nor do they considered themselves or the group to be ill. In their current environment, they believe that everyone is doing the same things; therefore, they are performing how they were designed at an optimal level. In this mode of thinking the opposite will also be considered true. Those who are not doing what we consider to be the norm are the ones considered sick or insane. I can remember we used to say things like "Man, fine as that girl is you are crazy if you wouldn't hit that." Implying that any normal person would have sex with any female whom they considered having a nice shape, and only an abnormal person would restrain their self and wait. We must understand that we have allowed the current moral state of our environment to determine normal versus abnormal. As a result, we call evil good, and on the contrary, we call godly thinking and behavior evil. What if we are created for a higher purpose? What if, what we are considering to be normal human behavior is totally different from our original design? The Word of GOD declares that every man's lifestyle is proper and upright in his own eyes and their own point of view. But the LORD weighs or judges as with a scale the inner man and the motives of the heart (Proverbs 21:2). Jesus said to the Pharisees "You are the ones who pronounce yourselves just and upright in the eyes of men; however, GOD knows your secret thoughts and desires. The things which are important or highly esteemed among men are despicable and evil in the eyes of GOD" (Luke 16:15).

Proverbs 21:2 (KJV)
Every way of a man is right in his own eyes: but the LORD pondereth the hearts.

Think about this, on a cardiac unit in a hospital, there are more people experiencing alterations in heart functions than there are individuals who do not have heart problems. What if the patients with congestive heart failure and myocardial infarctions believed they were the norm due to the number of people with these conditions? As a matter of fact, in that environment, they would be considered normal, and everyone else is abnormal and needs to change. With this mindset, all the patients experiencing congestive heart failure and heart attacks (myocardial infarctions) would refuse treatment because they are the norm and anyone with their condition that is seeking treatment because they want to change their current state would be looked down upon. That is the way it is in today's society. In some neighborhoods, children who use proper English are looked down on. Among some groups, individuals who do not smoke or drink are treated as if they are different. What about the virgins who feel like they are the only ones and that something is wrong with them? Just because something seems common, does not mean that it is okay. More people live in poverty than those that are considered to be wealthy; therefore, poverty is common. Regarding wealth and income, the bottom ninety percent of Americans are thought to hold approximately seventy-three percent of all debt in the United States; thus debt among the poor also is common. Now you tell me which group needs help, the wealthy or the poor. First Corinthians chapter ten verse thirteen declares, there is no temptation (intrinsic or extrinsic, regardless of where it comes from) has overtaken or enticed us except that which is common to the human existence. This passage of scripture goes on to state, just because the object of our enticement is common to the human experience; it is not beyond our ability to resist because of GOD's faithfulness. The LORD is faithful to His word; therefore, He will not allow us to be tempted beyond our ability to resist, but with every temptation, He will make a way of escape so that we can endure the temptation without surrendering to the pressure of the sinful desire.

Just because something seems common, does not mean that it is okay. Jesus said people that are in good health do not need a physician, only individuals who are sick. He also declared that he did not come to call or invite to repentance the righteous, but those who realize they are sinners and have a desire to be set free from the bondage of sin. (Matthew 9:12-13, Luke 5:31-32). Only if we confess our sins, has He (GOD) promised to forgive us and cleanse us of all our unrighteousness. We must understand, the fact that we feel that we were born with a desire or born a certain way does not justify our actions nor does our carnal desires right.

It is our duty to discern between what is normal to our carnal man but abnormal to our position with GOD. Furthermore, it is our responsibility to judge between what appears right in the eyes of man versus what is righteous in the eyes of GOD. We must understand that when our actions are consistent with what we deem as the majority of people, there is a level of comfort and as a result complacency sets in. It requires inward reflection and a glimpse of how things should be and not how things are commonly done to stir a desire to change. In the early 1900s, segregation was commonplace but Martin Luther King, Jr along with many others, before and after him, had a vision of how things should be and as a result; they began to fight against what was once considered the status quo or what was accepted as the norm. It is amazing to think that some African Americans felt as if any Black person having the same things as Whites were uppity. A friend of mine was the first black female director of pharmacy of a hospital located in a small town. Blacks had risen to levels of success in this area; thus, my friend was shocked when she heard some people saying, "She is going to have to learn her place." "She can't be telling those White folk what to do." In spite of the varying levels of success in this small town, Black people seeing themselves as less than was still common. This mindset is a direct result of mental pressure, and distress brought on by being subjected to unjust treatment or control for a prolonged period of time (oppression). Although, oppression can start with an external source the battle can become internal. This inner fight can become so stressful that it pushes us to the point of acceptance and conformity with an illegitimate mindset or thought process. Have ever heard someone say, "This is just the way that I am" as if they cannot or will not change? Have you ever did something that you were hesitant to do at first; however, once you did it became easier to do it again? There is an old saying, "One time is too many and a thousand times is not enough." The phrase "I would never" have been transformed into "everyone is doing it." Now it is no longer considered taboo but presented as common and accepted. All of this to say, just because something is common, does not mean that is right and just because something is good, does not mean that it is GOD.

Our human nature is common; however, many of its thoughts and actions are not righteous, and they are definitely not godly. The actions stemming from our fleshly nature are a direct result of the illness within our soul. In the beginning, GOD told Adam that if he ate of the tree of the knowledge of good and evil, he would surely die. The day Adam disobeyed GOD, he became mortally ill. Adam contracted a specific condition that prevents his mind and body from working the way that GOD originally intended. By one man's disobedience, everyone who is born from the seed of an earthly father has contracted or been infected with the same sin (Romans 5:12). Therefore, all have sinned and do fall short of the glory of GOD.

This state in the eyes of man is the new normal. If everyone has it or if everyone is doing it then it must be okay. The question becomes; why apologize for something that is a normal aspect of our human nature? The Scriptures declares that there is no strong urges or desires, which we experience in our carnal bodies that are not common to all humans. Everybody is doing it. Nobody is perfect. James (the brother of Jesus) tells us, GOD does not entice or causes anyone to sin, but we are all baited to commit actions that go against the will of GOD, because of the strong desires that are awakened in our fallen nature. This is why GOD gave so many great, precious, and costly promises that through His Word and the atoning sacrifice of Jesus Christ, we may live according to His divine nature and as a result, avoid the corruption that is in the world brought on by our carnal desires. GOD does not want us settling for a merely human existence when His original plan for a glorious life is available. He wants us to be transformed into a person with a different nature by changing the way we think (1Corinthians 10:13, James 1:13-14, 2Peter 1:4).

In the same way that our outward appearance impacts how we physically appear to others, our inner man or our soul influences how we see ourselves as well as how we assume others may see us. According to the book of Numbers the thirteenth chapter, the spies to told Moses that they were grasshoppers in our own sight, and therefore, they assumed that children of Anak saw them as mere insects as well. We have to learn to view ourselves differently before we can truly demand and expect others to see and treat us differently.

David was just a ruddy kid until he killed Goliath, and then his brothers saw him differently. When the prophet Samuel saw Jesse's son Eliab, he said to himself surely this is the LORD's anointed. Samuel thought this based on how Eliab carried himself as well as his outward appearance (height and stature). However, the LORD told Samuel not to look at the outward appearance to determine who will be chosen but to look at the heart (inner man, mind). The LORD also told the prophet, Jeremiah, that He searches the heart and tries the mind or the inner character, to give to every man according to their ways, and according to what they have done (1Samuel 16:6-7 and Jeremiah 17:10).

When the soul of man came to life so did his intellect, appetite, desires, and emotions. In Deuteronomy chapter twelve verse twenty, Moses told the children of Israel saying, "After the LORD GOD has fulfilled His promise enlarging your territory, and one day you say, 'I will eat meat,' because your soul desires to eat flesh. You may eat flesh, whatsoever your soul lusts after." As stated previously our body needs carbohydrates, proteins, and fats as well as other micronutrients for survival. It does not care if the protein came from the chicken or the egg, beans or peanuts; our body only desires the protein. As aforementioned, the body wants what it wants, and it does not care about who or what. When the flesh is stimulating and pushing the inner man to have sex, it does not care who or where; the flesh just wants what it wants. The carnal nature goes from one source to the next until it is satisfied. It is the soul of man that specifies who and where. It is the soul that desires and distinguishes between wanting chicken and steak. The body only desires sex. Question, do you only have one person in mind or do you have a list? Of course, you start at the top with your first choice but is that your only choice. This struggle might have started with the flesh, but has now become an internal issue. Notice, Moses did not say whatever your body craves, but rather whatsoever, your soul desires or lusts after. In Psalm forty-two the writer declared, "As the deer longs for water, so my soul longs for thee, O God. My soul thirsts for God, for the living God: when shall I come and appear before God?" Because our flesh cannot specify it cannot truly love in the sense of having a specific attraction to a particular person, place, or thing. The Apostle Paul admonishes us to follow after love but rather crave spiritual gifts. Our body does not care about being spiritual; therefore, this desire must come from within.

Song of Solomon 1:7
Tell me, O thou whom my soul loveth, where thou feedest, where thou makest thy flock to rest at noon: for why should I be as one that turneth aside by the flocks of thy companions?

Although, it is the spirit of man who gives the body life; it is the soul of man who gives the body emotion and character (life). If a person walks around and never shows any range of emotion, or they do not get excited about anything, we would consider that person to be dead (boring, lacking personality or emotion). They are not spiritually dead, nor physically deceased; however, they are emotionally lifeless. With this in mind, to understand truly, the soul of man, we must understand his mind, will, and emotions.

THE MATRIX OF THE MIND

The Word of God declares that GOD granted authority to man (blessed) by saying, be fruitful, multiply, replenish the earth, Subdue it, and have dominion. We must understand that this decree from GOD is no different from when He said, "Let there be light." The light had to come forth and present itself unto the LORD; it did not have a choice. If we notice in this first chapter of Genesis everything that GOD said had to come forth. His Word could not return to Him void or empty, but it had to accomplish and produce everything that GOD desired. GOD's Word must prosper (push forward, breakout, come, and be profitable) in the thing for which He (GOD) has sent it. Remember Jesus sent his word and healed the centurion's servant. The Word could not return without accomplishing healing. Thus, in this chapter, GOD was speaking what He wanted to see, and it was so; however, with man He used a different process. As stated in an earlier chapter GOD formed the body of man, and then He blew into man the breath of life; transforming man into a living soul. This is important to comprehend because GOD did not speak the blessing to man while he was a lifeless body. GOD waited for man to become a living soul before He spoke the blessing.

You see it is not the flesh, but the soul that GOD wants to empower to be and to do. In verse twenty-six of this first chapter, we find GOD having a conversation with Himself saying, "Let us make man in our image and after our likeness." Remember, our flesh is not in GOD's image nor His likeness. No flesh can glory or boast in His sight. It was the inner man whom the LORD wanted to empower or bless with the ability to be the image and likeness of the Almighty GOD. With all the other creatures that the LORD created, the pattern consisted of GOD saying, they came into being, and then GOD bless them. However, with man GOD discussed with Himself first, next He formed, He breathed, man became, and then GOD said. The LORD created man to be a spiritual being or personality.

Personality is defined as a personal existence. It is a set of complex characteristics or distinctive traits that distinguish an individual. Furthermore, personality relates to character, conduct, and motives of an individual. Thus, GOD empowered the character, conduct, and motives of man to "Be fruitful (bear fruit, cause to grow or increase, and bring forth), multiply (be or become great, become many, become numerous; to increase [in whatever respect]), replenish (fill the earth, fill until it is full), and subdue (to tread down; to conquer, keep under, bring into subjection and dominate) the earth! Having Dominion (to tread down, that is, subjugate, prevail against, reign, and be masters) over the fish in the ocean, the birds that fly, and every living thing that crawls on the earth." As a result, the desire to be fruitful, multiply, fill the earth until it is full, conquer it, and have dominion is hardwired to our human personality. When we are covered and lead by the Holy Spirit, we are able to find a balance; however, without the Spirit of GOD ruling in our hearts and mind, finding true stability is a never-ending roller-coaster ride. In our current fallen state we are never satisfied because we are always seeking to be fruitful (increase), and multiply (become great). After a few years on the job, we want a promotion either because we want more money or because we crave greater status. All of these desires or driving forces are not evil they are GOD given; however, in our current state, they are flesh driven. I think now is a good time to take a personal inventory of these five areas and determine if they are controlled by GOD or are they consistently stirred by your flesh. How faithful are you? Do you feel as if GOD has brought people in your life to help you get to the next level or are you supposed to help them? Do you feel as if you are supposed to submit and be fathered or mentored by someone else or do you have to be the leader? Are you trying to subdue and have dominion over GOD or are you allowing the Holy Spirit to have free reign and take control of you? Just pause for a few minutes and answer these questions honestly. Pray and ask the LORD to give clarity that you might see what He sees and that you bring your personality under subjection to the Spirit of GOD.

As human beings, it is also hardwired in our primary nature that we act to survive as an individual and as well as a species. Thus, our basic instincts are guided by our needs to preserve and prolong life, as well as prorogate. These human instincts become motivational forces that drive us to seek things such as food and water to alleviate hunger and thirst. At the same time, our human nature drives us to seek to continue the life of the species, by motivating or stirring our desire to have sex. Moreover, as a direct result of our need for survival, there is a basic need to avoid pain (physical or emotional). These natural predispositions are innate or intrinsic to our inner man and can be activated and agitated by our flesh. Remember the spirit does not get hungry or tired, and it does have a need to reproduce. All of these desires are turned on because our carnal man has needs. The problem with our nature is that these basic needs can become carnal wishes derived from want and not of necessity. Remember, we often eat desert after we have gotten full from our meal. In our carnal state our natural cravings can become insatiable. The Word of GOD compares the appetite or desires of man to that of hell, the grave, destruction, and even fire. The Word declares that as these cannot be satisfied neither cannot our fleshly desires. (Proverbs 30:15; Ecclesiastes 1:8; Ezekiel 16:29; Habakkuk 2:5). I do not need a new pair of shoes; nevertheless, I want some. I know that I have said, "I don't need that piece of cake, but I am going to eat this anyway."

Ecclesiastes 5:10 (KJV)
He that loveth silver shall not be satisfied with silver; nor he that loveth abundance with increase: this is also vanity.

The mind is the element of a person that enables them to be aware of the world and their experiences, to think, and to feel;

it is the inherent capability, power, function, and natural aptitude of human consciousness and thought. It holds the power of instincts, imagination, reason, recognition, and appreciation, and is responsible for processing what we see and hear. It is also responsible for our feelings and emotions, which in turn influences our attitudes and actions. The mind can be divided into two basic levels of consciousness or level of awareness (what is happening around us specific to our environment and time). These levels of awareness are divided into our conscious and subconscious (unconscious) mind. The conscious mind contains or deals with information that we are aware of at any given moment. The conscious mind consists of our present perceptions, superficial memories, thoughts, ideas, and feelings. The subconscious mind is considered to be the largest area of the mind and is thought to be the seat of our innate or intrinsic motivations, whether they be desires for food, water, sex, or compulsion that is brought on by fear or anxiety. The unconscious mind includes all the things that are not easily available to our awareness; it is the place where hidden or deeply seated memories and emotional traumas that we do not want to remember are stored. These concealed issues and traumas may not reach the level of mental alertness; however, these are the unconscious things that will cause us to act without thinking. The subconscious mind is thought to be the only component of human personality (character) that is present and completely active from birth. The subconscious mind is very important to newborn and young children early in life because they cannot clearly communicate their needs or desires; therefore, the unconscious mind pushes them to act or respond until their needs are met. Thus, if the baby is hungry or uncomfortable, it will cry until it is feed or its diaper is changed. There is no reasoning with them, in other words, their conscious mind is not working; therefore, it is not about what they think it is all about what they want. How do you know when the baby is full or satisfied? When it stops crying? With our conscious mind, we can reason and make decisions; however, with our subconscious mind, we do not think we just react. In the midst of conflict, we can choose how we want to respond based on the fact that we have learned how to control our natural desires. However, if we become too emotional or the pressure of the conflict is constant and intense enough it can chip away and break our ability to prevent or control a deep-seated reaction. Whatever is stored deep within our subconscious mind can push us into responding in a way that we initially did not want to. What if we have not been working on self-control? In that situation, our first response will probably always be the undesired action. We will find ourselves constantly in a place of feeling bad because of what we have done.

The Word of GOD declares in first Samuel chapter twenty-four verse four that David's conscience bothered him, and his heart was full of regret because he had cut off Saul's skirt. David realized that he was not acting to honor the LORD, but rather to satisfy an inward desire to get the one that was trying to attack him. I can remember a time before my unit participated in Operation Desert Storm, I was an easy-going person. At least to me anyway. If my friends in the Marine Corps were about to get into a fight, I would often times be the voice of reason. However, I can distinctly remember while I was in Saudi when one of my friends asked, "Scott, what is wrong with you?" In my mind, I am thinking nothing. He goes on to say, "You used to be the one that would stop us from fighting, and now we are the ones that have to stop you. You have changed!" It was then that I realized that I was anxious, and my will to survive pushed me into a defensive mindset. In my subconscious mind, I was going to fight or kill you before you killed me. However, it was not because I was a tough guy. It was my unconscious mind pushed me to do what I have seen others do, and I did not even recognize it.

The conscious mind works to maintain a balance between stresses that are placed on us from reality and society versus the pressures that come from our internal drives natural instincts, or human desires. When the desire that originates from without clashes with the desires from within, we begin to feel overwhelmed or anxious. These feelings or emotions that create anxiety in our inner man serve as an alert sent from our consciousness that our survival is in danger. Remember, the survival mechanism is hardwired into our human nature. Thus, whether we realize it or not we are going to respond to every threat. Our unconscious mind will push us to deny (blocking external events from awareness), fight, avoid, or escape the stimuli that are stirring our survival mechanisms. Often times on a daily basis we are unconsciously blocking or distorting urges that may cause us to feel threatened or emotional.

Avoidance is a common tool used by our inner man. Many people avoid going to the doctor because they are trying to avoid receiving bad or depressing news. Have you ever found yourself trying to avoid someone? Why are you avoiding them? Avoidance is not only the act of keeping away from or withdrawing from someone or something undesirable; it is a pro-active response carried out to avoid a deleterious stimulus. Stimuli do not have to deal with anger alone, but can cover a multitude of areas. I have seen individuals that were so sexually attracted to another person that they literally avoided them. I mean they would not even talk to them. Not only do we actively avoid others; we avoid dealing with our own shortcoming. Often times we confuse avoidance with abstinence, and we confuse abstinence with deliverance. We must understand avoiding a stimulus does not mean that we have developed the power to abstain. Can you say, "No" when you are face to face with the temptation? And just because we have learned how to say, "No" does not mean that we have lost our desire for it. I have heard individuals who thought they were delivered from drugs say, one morning they woke up with a craving. Remember, being in the flesh means to have weakness ever present. The Apostle Paul said, he found a law at work in his inner man that when he would do good, evil was always present.

I have heard it said, "Nothing beats a failure but a try." However, several people are so terrified of failure; they never try. Many people will say that they are not ready to give their lives to Christ because they are still struggling in their flesh. They are afraid to fail GOD and ultimately themselves. Remember, fear often triggers our survival mechanisms. This internal anxiety can result in emotions so powerful that we become frozen, unable to move toward success. Some individuals begin to consider suicide as a mechanism to avoid dealing with the internal conflicts that are warring in their mind resulting in great emotional pain. When we are afraid of what may or may not happen, we doom ourselves to fail. Often times we subconsciously run away from our success as an act of avoidance not wanting to face the emotional pain of possibly failing. Failure is not an option; it is the result of incorrect actions or the lack of acting altogether, because of what is going on in our mind.

THE LAW OF REQUISITE VARIETY

Have you ever heard of the Law of Requisite Variety? It states that the system with the most flexibility of behavior will control or have the most influence on its environment. This is also known as the first law of Cybernetics. The word cybernetics comes from a Greek word, and it basically means to govern or to control, direct, or strongly influence the actions and conduct of living things as well as machines or electronics. One example of a cybernetic system is how the brain and central nervous system (CNS) controls our mood as well as our actions based on the influence of the outside environment. One of the most basic and common examples of a cybernetic system is a thermostat that is concerned with the ambient temperature of its environment. A thermostat is designed to sense the room temperature and control the A/C unit causing it to turn on and off. The thermostat is a very simple system while the brain and CNS are more complex. In general, the more complicated the system and its processes are the larger the number of variables that are associated with it.

To put it another way, complex systems must be able to deal with a greater variety of disturbances or conflicts than simple systems. The law of requisite variety governs the capacity or aptitude of a control system to respond to the various challenges that can occur in its environment. This law is a quantitative statement about the diverse types of responses a system needs to have available to deal with the varied range of disturbances that it might experience. To say it another way the law of requisite variety states, that the greater the variety of actions available to a regulatory system, the larger the variety of alterations in the normal state (trepidations) the control system is able to compensate for. When the control system is given multiple options on how to establish balance when facing a deviation in the normal state, the control system has the ability to select the appropriate response so that equilibrium and control are preserved. Would you feel nervous about an exam if you knew beforehand the variations of each question that the professor could possibly ask? How anxious would you feel if you not only knew the variations of the test questions, but you also had the answers to each question? When a control mechanism has the correct response to a potential stressor, anxiety is avoided, and the system stays in balance.

We are creatures of habit, and our bodies work tirelessly to maintain homeostasis or a normal balance. Anything that disturbs this balance or when our control or compensatory mechanisms cease to respond, disease (physical, mental, etc.) or behavioral changes may occur. For example, our bodies work to maintain acid/base balance; therefore, if our control system is working appropriately when our bicarb levels decrease our breathing will automatically change increasing the rate at which we breathe off acid (CO_2). As a result of this compensation, metabolic acidosis is avoided and the patient may not perceive that anything is wrong or out of balance. A system that provides several options for maintaining normalcy appears to be stress-free. This does not mean that disturbances are not occurring but rather the control system has the ability to compensate for those conflicts or change what is considered normal. Society itself is one of the greatest and most complex examples of a cybernetic system. In society, we have control systems and variable for each individual, for groups, and all aspects and interactions existing in society. When examining interactions between individuals or groups, we find that individuals or groups with the highest amount of flexibility of behavior will have the most influence on the system. For example, what if you were hungry and the closest restaurant is ten miles away? Two variables may cause stress to the system; hunger and distance to the restaurant. What if there was only one restaurant, and it closes in twenty minutes, does the variables that place pressure on the system increase? Yes, because it assumes that the number of options that are available to the control mechanism responsible for dealing with the stress of hunger are few. Do you have a car? Are you driving or do have to rely on someone else?

The more questions or disturbances that exist within the system that lack a proper response by our control system will result in increased stress or pressure on the system as a whole. However, if you could increase the number of appropriate responses that balance the system; the stress will diminish or be eliminated altogether. For example, the restaurant you want closes in twenty minutes; however, there are ten others that will remain open for another four hours. All of the restaurants are in walking distance, and you also have four cars to choose from. You see, the greater the level of flexibility or the greater the variety of choices available to an individual, group, or society the greater the liberty and the better quality of life. This takes us back to the statement that individuals or groups with the highest amount of flexibility of behavior will have the most influence on the system. This is one reason why many minorities want to assimilate or become like the majority race because it appears as if certain ethnic groups have greater flexibility of behavior. It is not because one group is better than another, but rather one group appears to have several options for maintaining normalcy. As a result, their lives appear to be stress-free. This is also true with non-Christians, carnal Christians, and overcoming Christians. Individuals who are really trying to live a life pleasing to GOD seem to struggle emotionally because they often fall short. As a result, a great amount of pressure and stress is placed on the individual. These feelings of guilt and fear will send them into survival mode. We must remember that we are a work in progress, and the Spirit of GOD is going to continue to work on us right up to the day of His return.

Because of Adam's disobedience, we were placed in bondage to sin. We have a desire to be set free; however, the freedom that most people are looking for is to be free from bondage with all rights and privileges to do whatever we want, whenever we want. We want freedom with all-encompassing liberty without the restraints. Remember a system that provides several options for maintaining normalcy appears to be stress-free, and it is in our basic human nature to desire to be anxiety free. Again, this does not mean that carnal desires or disturbances are not occurring but rather our flesh (the control system) wants to have the ability to compensate for those conflicts by doing whatever is necessary to satisfy those disturbances or change what is considered normal in order to remove the stress of wanting what we want. The law of requisite variety allows the control system to make up rules as it goes to adapt to the various disturbances that occur in an environment. The first law of cybernetics is about control or influence; however, when applied liberally in society or in the Church it will actually bring about a lack of control. It will create an environment where there is a consistent lowering of our moral standards merely to keep down stress and strife. The social control theory suggests that a person's relationships, obligations, values, norms, and beliefs will inspire them not to break the law. However, if what is considered the norm is outside of the confines of the moral law, the same will be true. Many others will begin to follow; hence, one of the strategies of the enemy is to bombard us with something creating the illusion that it is commonplace and good when in actuality, it is evil. We then allow the perceived majority to set the rules for what is considered the new normal. Consequently, if the moral codes of the community become non-existent or erroneous individuals within that group will begin to make connections with the abnormal behaviors in their community or neighborhoods; thus, voluntarily become more deviant, and their propensity to commit sin in the eyes of GOD will increase.

Often times when we have been in bondage for long periods of time, it becomes difficult to understand and utilize all the liberties that we have been granted. In the movie "The Shawshank Redemption" the character "Red" kept asking his supervisor for a restroom break even though he had the liberty to go at any time. In the same way that Red did not recognize the liberty that he had as a result of his new-found freedom, most believers do not understand the liberty that we have in Christ. Christ declared, the Spirit of the LORD was upon him to set at liberty them that are bruised or to deliver and set free those that have been oppressed. Galatians chapter five verse one admonishes us to enjoy the benefits and stand firmly in the freedom that Christ has given to us. It also admonishes us not to be entangled again with the yoke of bondage. In verse thirteen of this same chapter, Paul is cautioning us as believers not allow our new freedom to become an occasion or opportunity for the carnal nature of our flesh to act out of control. In the Holy Scriptures, we see the words freedom and liberty. Many of us do not understand the difference between freedom and liberty. We are set free from something and given liberty (the right or power) to do something. Liberty tells us what we have the right or ability to do; which we can then infer that there must be some things that we cannot do. We have been set free from the bondage of sin and granted the liberty to walk in the newness of life. A new life that is free of sickness and poverty. However, we cannot let our freedom go to our head causing us to become prideful and committing presumptuous sins by overstepping our bounds taking liberties that have not been given to us (Psalm 19:13, 1Corinthians 8:9-13).

CHANGING THE WAY WE THINK

Romans 12:2 (NLT)
Don't copy the behavior and customs of this world, but let God transform you into a new person by changing the way you think. Then you will learn to know God's will for you, which is good and pleasing and perfect.

As we discuss the mind or intellect of man, I feel it is necessary to define a few words that I believe will help us to understand where we are as well as where we need to be. The first word is science. Science is defined as the state of having systematized knowledge or a state of knowing. It is knowledge covering general truths or the operation of general laws. Secondly, is the word philosophy, and it is basically a rule of thought, point of view, or system of beliefs. Common synonyms we used in place of philosophy or philosophical are theory or theoretical (hypothetical and speculative), Truth-seeking, and idealistic. Thirdly, is the word psychology, and it is essentially a mindset in which a point of view or system of beliefs is developed. It is the mental or behavioral characteristics of an individual or group. Our psychology can help to develop our philosophy. Lastly, is the word psychosomatic, and it involves both mind and body. It deals with the relationship between bodily actions or symptoms caused by our mental or emotional state. These terms are important to understand because the study of our soul (mind, personality, character, and behavior) is still very much philosophical in the sense that understanding exactly what we are going to do and why is still hypothetical or abstract. We may be able to identify and narrow down the options; however, we do not know definitively what a person is going to do until they do it. Thus, some argue that psychology is not scientific. The mental processes are very abstract and are constantly in a state of dynamic interaction. Hence, the laws in psychology are not as exact and precise as those in physics. With that being said, most people have predictable patterns of behavior. Especially if the behavior is a reflexive act (psychosomatic) stemming from our subconscious mind. Often times, in the church many leaders argue and disagree because they have different philosophies (rules of thought, points of view, or system of beliefs). Philosophy is the pursuit of wisdom as well as the search for a general understanding by predominantly theoretical means. You will find that there is philosophy (points of view, truth-seeking) in religion; however, GOD does not argue philosophy. In GOD, there is only one truth and only one point of view, and it is His. The Word of GOD declares that Christ Jesus is the truth, and His point of view is the only one that matters. Let the morally wrong forsake their ways, and the unrighteous person their thoughts. Because my thoughts are not your thoughts, neither are your ways my ways, says the LORD. Even as the heavens are higher than the earth, so are my ways higher than your ways, and my thoughts than your thoughts (Isaiah 55:7-9).

Furthermore, you will find that there is a science to the bible. However, you will never have GOD down to a science. In GOD, the same methods (steps) may not yield the same results at the same time. Because GOD considers the intent of our heart as well as the times and seasons just as much as He considers the results of our actions. Sowing and reaping is a law that works the same way every time; however, when or how long it takes to see a harvest from the seeds that have been sown is another question. Two people may be praying the same prayer; however, one gets results and the other nothing. In the Gospel of Matthew the twenty-sixth chapter, we find Jesus praying the same prayer three times. So it is not the number of times you pray the identical prayer that makes it vain, but rather the state of your heart. You see the method may be the same, but the results or timing may vary (James 5:15-18; Matthew 6:5-8). More than philosophy and science there is psychology all throughout the bible. A part of building faith is the changing or renewing of the mind.

GOD wants us to let the mind of Christ operate through us in our daily lives (Philippians 2:5). Maturing in our minds concerning the spiritual things of GOD is an important part of our spiritual growth (1Corinthians 3:1-3; Hebrew 5: 12:13). We must allow the peace (prosperity, oneness, quietness, and rest) of God to have dominion and rule in our hearts (Colossians 3:15). Remember, the carnal mind cannot receive the things of GOD. The carnal mind is not subject to the law of GOD (Romans 8:1-14). GOD uses different situations and circumstances to show himself and pull down strongholds in our lives. GOD knows that if we change the way we think about ourselves, others, and life; we can change the way we live all together.

In life, much of what we think we know about ourselves, others and life, in general, is based upon prejudices, biases, and opinions that we have picked up over the years. Most of our knowledge concerning others is based on the assumptions or norms that we developed to categorize and understand their actions. The Word of GOD declares that the LORD spoke to Moses personally, just as a man would speak with his friend. And yet we find Moses asking, "LORD to teach me your ways that I might know you and become more deeply and intimately acquainted with you (Exodus 33:11-13). Moses seemed to have understood that in order to receive more favor from the LORD, he must become more intimate with the person of GOD. Moses needed to know not just what GOD has done, is doing, or going to do. He must understand why. Understanding why leads us to the place of understanding the mind of GOD and not merely the actions of GOD. Psalm one-hundred-three verse seven states that GOD revealed his ways to Moses and his acts to the people of Israel. The Scriptures declare the depth of the richness of GOD's wisdom and knowledge; exclaiming that God's decisions are mysterious, inexplicable, and unsearchable and His ways are past finding out! The Apostle Paul asked a question, who has known the mind (the intellect as well as the divine thoughts, feelings, and divine will) of the LORD (Romans 11:33-34)? As stated earlier, it is the glory of God to conceal a thing, but the glory and honor of kings is to search it out (Proverb 25:2). This leaves us with a problem. If the judgments and ways of the LORD are inscrutable, and they are far above our natural capacity for wisdom and understanding. How do we in our earthly mindset obtain true glory and honor? We cannot understand the mind and ways of GOD without help. This is why the Apostle Paul desired that our faith be securely rooted in the power of GOD and not in the wisdom and philosophy of man nor of the demonic power (princes) of this world (1Corinthians 2:7-16). In order to see into the mind of GOD and gain understanding, we must become more intimate with the person of GOD and not have casual communication with Him. Just because you have seen me, or because we have talked on different occasions does not mean that you truly know me or are able to see into me (in-to-me-see). One way in which intimacy can be developed is through intercourse. As aforementioned, true intercourse is not sex but communication. It is a connection or an exchange of intimate thoughts or feelings between two or more individuals. Penetration occurs as a result of positive and effective communication. The word penetrate means to gain access or enter by overcoming resistance.

Furthermore, it means to see into or through; to discover the inner contents or meaning of. This is powerful because when we have effective intercourse with the LORD, we finally get to the place where we are truly open to surrender, allowing Him to penetrate our heart and mind filling us with His Word and His Spirit. The power of daily communication will lead to us becoming impregnated with GOD's purpose. When we become pregnant with purpose, we do not have to try to figure out what to do. We just need to give birth. Another way to develop intimacy is through common experiences. The seventeenth chapter of the book of Proverbs verse seventeen declares that a friend is one that loves at all times, and they become more like a brother during times of adversity. We see this all the time in sports. The coaches work to create an environment of hardships and difficulty in an attempt to bond the players together creating a more cohesive unit. For most of us, it is during times of distress when we call the LORD early and often. We want to have communion with Him every day. Through consistent communication and common experiences, we develop a sense of closeness, understanding, and a true relationship.

1Corinthians 2:11, 14-16 (KJV)
Vs14 But the natural man receiveth not the things of the Spirit of God: for they are foolishness unto him: neither can he know them, because they are spiritually discerned. Vs15 But he that is spiritual judgeth all things, yet he himself is judged of no man. Vs16 For who hath known the mind of the Lord, that he may instruct him? But we have the mind of Christ.

Much like the ways of GOD, understanding how we think and why we do the things we do has proven to be an enigma to mankind. When we attempt to study the mind or more precisely the personality, character, and behavior of man, one thing becomes evident. The study of the mind from a humanistic view is very subjective (prejudiced, skewed). It involves assessing things that are only available to the person (i.e., your inner thoughts and feelings) by systematically judging their actions. The Apostle Paul asked the question, "What person knows and understands the true motives of a man?" Paul goes on to say, no man utilizing human ability can discern these motives except his own spirit that is within him (1Corinthians 2:11). Because our natural man cannot comprehend spiritual things, and our ability to assess what is in the mind or heart of an individual is predicated solely on the actions or manifestations of the individual. We must remember that every action begins as a thought; therefore, from the abundance of the heart, the mouth will speak. Furthermore, a tree is identified and judged by its fruit. (Matthew 12:33).

Years ago, my uncle gave my cousin an orange tree, so he said. To them, it looked like an orange tree. They planted and nurtured the tree waiting for it to produce some oranges. However, when the tree was able to produce fruit, it produced grapefruits. My uncle thought for sure that he picked out an orange tree, but the tree did not care what he consciously thought, it produced what was in its roots. Even though it might have looked like an orange tree, at the root (in its heart), there was a grapefruit. In our carnal state, the only way to assess truly what is going through our mind is through our actions. But do we always do what we consciously think? Furthermore, just because every action begins as a thought that does not mean that we are truly aware of our every thought. Remember some of our actions are considered to be psychosomatic or a subconscious reflex. Some of our actions we do not know, neither do we understand why we did what we did or said what we said. Some thoughts are not accessible or available, to our conscious mind. With that being said, have you ever asked someone "why did you do that"? Better yet, have you ever asked yourself that question? This demonstrates another problem with studying the mind from a human or mortal point of view, and it is that our actions sometimes escape our own mind; therefore, it is difficult to associate a particular mindset with an outward action. I know what I did, but I cannot tell you why. Have you ever lied about something and then asked yourself "why did I lie"? The book of Jeremiah chapter seventeen verses nine and ten declares that the heart (the feelings, the will and the intellect) of man is deceitful and polluted above all things, and it cannot be searched out by man. The Scriptures asks the question, "Who can perceive and discern what is in his own heart?" It is the LORD who searches and intimately examines our hearts. Remember, everything that man thinks is good is not always GOD and just because something seems right according to our human way of life does not mean that it is righteous to GOD.

Mark 7:20-23 (KJV)
Vs20 And he said, That which cometh out of the man, that defileth the man. Vs21 For from within, out of the heart of men, proceed evil thoughts, adulteries, fornications, murders, Vs22 Thefts, covetousness, wickedness, deceit, lasciviousness, an evil eye, blasphemy, pride, foolishness: Vs23 All these evil things come from within, and defile the man.

As humans, we are predominately defined by what we do; however, with GOD our inner man defines us; therefore, He examines our heart, judges our words as well as our actions. GOD knows what is leading and motivating us; consequently, He focuses on the origin or the driving forces within and not merely the acts that occur as a result. The Scriptures declare that the Word of GOD is quick, and powerful, and sharper than any two-edged sword, penetrating to the dividing of the soul and spirit, and it discerns the thoughts and intents of the heart. Our reason for doing whatever we do is important to GOD. He wants to be the reason we sing, smile, work, and everything else. Whatever we do; the LORD wants us to do it from our soul, as unto Him, and not to please men.

Colossians 3:17 (KJV)
And whatsoever ye do in word or deed, do all in the name of the Lord Jesus, giving thanks to God and the Father by him.

The Apostle Paul wrote the Corinthians saying, "If I give all my goods to feed the poor, but it is not motivated by love; my actions will not have any true value." Our saying a thing is not the same as doing the thing. Our word should be our bond. Our yes should be yes, and our no should be no; however, with humans, this not always the case. Question, does our accomplishing what we said demonstrate the motivations of the heart? The answer to that question is simple; "not necessarily." This is why The LORD tries our heart to see what manner of man we are. For with our mouths, we can say that we are close to GOD; however, at the same time, our hearts can be far from Him. The Bible declares that many will say to the LORD, "have we not prophesied in your name, and in your name we have cast out devils? Have we not done many miracles and works that inspire wonder in your name?" Christ said that he would profess unto them, he never knew them and command that they depart from him. Christ banished them from his presence because they were workers of iniquity, from their hearts they transgressed against the law of Christ (Isaiah 29:13; Jeremiah 9:8; Matthew 7:22-23). You can say you love Christ, or you can say you love another person, but that which is rooted in your heart will manifest. Therefore, it is not merely about what we say, it is about what we do. And it is not solely based on what we say and do, it is also based on the intents of our heart. Remember, as a man thinks in his soul so is he. Question, what if your friend lies to you? What if they told you that your outfit looked great, but on the inside, they are saying, "What in the world"? Now let me ask you another question, is that friend a liar? Do you feel like they had malice in their heart because they lied to you on that occasion? What if they were worried about your feelings? Please understand that a lie is a lie and wrong is wrong, but we must be able to judge the words, deeds, and the intent of the inner man. Have you ever heard someone say, "GOD knows my heart." They usually say that after they have done something that is considered jacked up. Instead of them truly admitting they are wrong, they say "GOD knows my heart." As to say, forget how you feel and forget what everyone else thinks. Just because we started out with good in our hearts does not mean that we will not be judged based on our actions. GOD does know our heart;

however, it does not give us the right to continue in sin (Romans 6:1). This leads us back to the point; merely because something is done with good intentions does mean that it meets GOD standards. Our good intention on our best day is still considered filthy rags when compared to His righteousness. Whenever we do anything that falls short of GOD's glory, no matter what our initial intent was, we should repent quickly. We should not condemn ourselves, but rather ask for forgiveness and keep moving forward. We must understand that our falling short of demonstrating our love for the Father or for one another on occasion does not completely mean that our feelings or our hearts are against them. However, what this shows is that at the root of our carnal nature is the appetite or proclivity for sin. The Scriptures Declare The Law was given to us that we might know and recognize sin, and that sin might become exceedingly sinful. While we are in the flesh, the emotions and influences of sins work in our human nature to produce actions that lead to death. To deny our wrong or to say that we have not sinned is to call GOD a liar. Therefore, we must repent and deal with these areas in our flesh quickly before they grow out of control.

It is amazing how often we feel as if we already know all the answers concerning ourselves or our personality. It is true; we have direct access to our own thoughts and feelings, as well as plenty of experience dealing with people. However, we are confusing familiarity (acquaintance, awareness) with true knowledge (understanding, comprehension). In most instances, we are familiar with or aware of our actions in our everyday situations. As a result, it becomes easy for us to say what we think we would do in a situation. Have you ever heard someone say, "If I was you or if that was me?" Many of us make that statement as if we know exactly what we would do. However, if the truth be told most times we do not know what we would do because we do not truly know who we are and how we think subconsciously. Having true knowledge of our subconscious mind comes from understanding why we react the way we do as well as having the ability to control those same reactions. When I was in basic training for the United States Marine Corps, one of the recruits got caught sleeping while on watch. As a result, his face ran into a moonbeam. Another recruit saw this, and during a later conversation made the statement, "If that were me, I would...." About a week later while we were marching as a platoon, my friend got in serious trouble. He did not recognize our Drill Instructor's (DI) voice and started marching at the sound of another DI's voice. As a result, his face ran into our DI's backhand. I asked him later what did he do and of course, he did nothing. Why didn't he react the way he thought he would? Because down on the inside we were all terrified of the Drill Instructors. With his mouth, he was brave, and He may have actually acted tough or brave in common everyday situations outside of basic training. However, when we are in the midst of inner conflict or pressure that which is embedded deep within our subconscious mind, will always come out unless we develop the ability to make a conscious decision to change the outward response. Think about this. If a person is struggling with fornication, does this mean that in their mind, they love sex? We pray against fornication and never deal with the fact that in their subconscious mind, there is the root of rejection or abandonment. Sexual intercourse is merely the outward response that they use to feel intimate and connected to others. You see in this example even the individual with the problem may never relate their actions with rejection and abandonment, and if you were to ask them what was in their mind (heart), they might answer "I don't know I guess I just like it." What they do not understand is that it is not the sex, but the attention and temporary companionship associated with the sex that they need, crave and are ultimately seeking. In many addictions and phobias, the root causes are hidden deep within the subconscious mind; therefore, the conscious mind of the individual does not have access to his own true thoughts. Thus, sometimes we are familiar with what we will do and the superficial thoughts that appear to be consistent with our action, however, we do not have a clue of the deep thoughts that determine our personality or our ultimate actions. Only GOD truly knows what is in our hearts.

John 2:23-25 (AMP)
Now when He was in Jerusalem at the Passover feast, many believed in His name [identifying themselves with Him] after seeing His signs (attesting miracles) which He was doing. Vs24 But Jesus, for His part, did not entrust Himself to them, because He knew all people [and understood the superficiality and fickleness of human nature], Vs25 and He did not need anyone to testify concerning man [and human nature], for He Himself knew what was in man [in their hearts--in the very core of their being].

ZOOMED IN AND FOCUSED

Ezekiel 20: 7 (KJV)
Then said I unto them, Cast ye away every man the abominations of his
eyes, and defile not yourselves with the idols of Egypt: I am the LORD your
GOD.

Most of our struggles in life begin when we lose focus or sight of GOD and His plans for our lives. We begin to gaze at or contemplate what we want, think, or feel. Basically, we focus on self, becoming selfish instead of being selfless. Isaiah twenty-six verse three declared that the LORD would keep us in perfect peace if we keep our purpose, imagination, and mind focused on Him. Our mind uses our eyes like the camera uses its lens; therefore, I think it is important for us to understand the difference between being focused and zoomed in. Focusing is the process of adjusting the picture, so the desired object looks sharp or clear; while zooming is the process of narrowing the field of view to bring distant objects into view or to increase the magnification of the object. Zooming in will change the focus; however, being focused does not mean that we are zoomed in.

Once we are zoomed in, there is a decrease in the number of items that can be seen in the view, but it increases the detail in what we see if we are focused. When we are zoomed in and focused on a particular item, other objects may be in the picture, but they are blurred. If we are focused but zoomed out, we can see the big picture, but we lack clarity or details. However, when we are zoomed in we see the minute details, but to a very small piece of the puzzle. A picture taken from an airplane high above a metropolitan area can show all the tall buildings; however, it will not show the streets or the people walking around. When we apply this information to our inner man, we should be able to establish in our mind if we are in a state being focused, zoomed or both. It is important for us to understand that we cannot truly focus on multiple objects at one time if we desire clarity or detail, accuracy, and consistency. It is difficult for a person that is a spouse, parent, pastor, child, employee, administrator, sibling, aunt or uncle, and friend, to focus on all of these areas unless they are not zoomed in. In our carnal mindset, we usually zoom in on one aspect and blur the others. They are in the picture, but we cannot really see them. Remember focusing with a wide view brings everyone or everything into our view so that we can say I see you, but do we really see their intimate needs. Can you honestly give one-hundred percent of yourself to multiple tasks at the same time? Our mind is powerful to the tool, but much like a computer, when we leave too many windows open, over time, our ability to process begins to slow down. This is why we have to learn how to close some of the pages and be zoomed and focused on the moment at hand. When we are with our family, we must be zoomed and focused. Work may be in the background, but it is blurred. When we are at work, our minds must be locked in and engaged with the priorities of the job. This can be a daunting task, this why it is so important to learn self-management along with mastering time management. Self-management teaches us that there is simply one of us; therefore, we cannot give more than a hundred percent of our effort because we are one in our mind, will, and emotions. If you feel like you gave one-hundred-twenty percent today, that means what you thought was your best yesterday was only eighty percent of your total effort. Remember, at most, we can only give one-hundred percent of ourselves anything beyond that is not natural but supernatural. We must train our inner man to divide time and not itself.

The Word of GOD declares that a false balance is an abomination. A balance is a scale (literal or figurative) that is used to measure money (gold and silver), time, and effort. We must weigh our time in the balance and divide it appropriately and give a hundred percent of ourselves to that allotted time. When we get home from work if we only have three hours before the children go to bed; we must commit a hundred percent of ourselves to be locked in and engaged with them. Initially, work may still be in the background, but it is blurred. However, as we continue to zoom in and focus on our children, work seems to disappear. When we do that we do not have to worry about doing extra tomorrow because we gave them all we had at that time today. We may question the amount of time that we give, but we should never question the effort of our soul. Often times we lose focus and zoom when it comes to the things of GOD. He is there in the background, but we can barely see Him because things have gotten so hazy. Jesus told the disciples that anyone who hears the Word of GOD but allows the worries of the world and the deceitfulness of riches to distract them (taking their focus) is same as, the person that received seed among the thorns and thistles. It initially started to produce; however, distractions got in the way and choked it out before it produced fruit. David loss focus because he zoomed in on Bathsheba.

Solomon lost focus because of his desire for wisdom and women. Samson lost focus because he had zoomed in on Delilah, and it was only when he lost his eyes that he regained focus on what the LORD called him to do. I thank GOD that Jesus did not zoom out or lose focus on what the FATHER called him to do. Jesus also said to his disciples, I have a baptism to be baptized with; and how am I preoccupied (lost in thought) until it is accomplished (Luke 12:50). The LORD was so zoomed in and focused on the task at hand that when his flesh wanted less than what was required He said, nevertheless, and gave it all. Most of us find ourselves pulled over on the side of the road of life because we have lost focus, or we are zoomed in on the wrong things. The LORD is the only one that says, if we zoom in and focus on Him, putting first things first, He will cause all of these other things to come within our view with great details. Remember, Isaiah twenty-six verse three declared that the LORD would keep us in perfect peace (completeness or wholeness) if we keep our purpose, imagination, and mind focused on Him.

Our eyes are like the lens on the camera; however, we can only see what our mind allows us to see. Have you ever been walking and someone is trying to get your attention, but you do not see let alone hear them even though they are in plain sight? Your response is, "I am sorry I did not see you; my mind was somewhere else." Your eyes were opened yet your mind was not focused on them because it zoomed in somewhere else. Therefore, you could not see things outside of your frame of mind. Our eyes are important because they gather the information and sends it to our brain which in turn interprets the information and determines what you see. But no matter how well your eyes work if your mind refuses or rejects the information you will not see the object ever. Are you focused, zoomed in or both? Most of us prefer to walk through life zoomed out because of lack of trust. Remember, when we are zoomed in we can see more detail but a smaller piece of the picture. We believe that GOD has called us to start a business and by faith, we see ourselves walking in great success. We begin our journey zoomed in and focused on the success; however, after five years have passed, and we have trial after trial we think to ourselves GOD did not show us the big picture. As a result, we attempt to widen our view trying to see the big picture with thought any detail. In other words, we can see our beginning, and we have hope for our ending; however, we still cannot see with any detail what is going on the in the middle (the process). The Apostle Paul admonishes us in the book of Philippians to engage our will power and focus. Focus on whatsoever things are true, whatsoever things are honest, whatsoever things are just, whatsoever things are pure, whatsoever things are lovely, whatsoever things are of good report; if there be any virtue, and if there be any praise, focus and continually think on these things. The Amplified Bible tells us to center our mind on them, and implant them in our heart (Philippians 4:8). We must learn to trust in the LORD with all of our heart and lean not to our own understanding because He sees the big picture from the finish to the start with great clarity and detail of what will happen in the middle. If we keep the faith and acknowledge Him in all of our ways He will order our steps and direct our path. Much like the military GOD wants us to move according to his cadence. We must be in step with the LORD sensing His tempo and using it to keep us in alignment and moving in perfect unison as one unit or one body.

Matthew 6:21-24
For where your treasure is, there will your heart be also. Vs22 The light of the body is the eye: if therefore thine eye be single, thy whole body shall be full of light. Vs23 But if thine eye be evil, thy whole body shall be full of darkness. If therefore the light that is in thee be darkness, how great is that darkness! Vs24 No man can serve two masters: for either he will hate the one, and love the other; or else he will hold to the one, and despise the other. Ye cannot serve God and mammon.

NOT MY WILL BUT THY WILL BE DONE

Our mind is the battleground where the desires of GOD meet the desires of our carnal nature in a fight for our obedience and ultimately our soul. The Bible declares that the law of sin which, works in our flesh is at war against the law of GOD, which works in our mind. The law at work in our godless human nature tries to get us to yield to sin, while the law at work in our mind wants us to obey GOD. We must understand that there is a mutual hatred/enmity between the carnal mind and law of GOD and we are servants to whomever we yield ourselves. While in a place called Gethsemane, Jesus stated that is his soul (psuche) was exceedingly sorrowful and as a result Jesus prayed the same prayer three times "Father, if it be possible let this cup pass from me; nevertheless, not as I will, but as thou wilt (Matthew 26:36-44 KJV). There were two options in front of Jesus, the will of his flesh or the will of GOD (his Father). Jesus' desire to please and fulfill the will of his Father caused him to say not my will but Father your will be done. The word "will" can be used to express desire, choice, willingness, capability or sufficiency. It also can be used to express determination, insistence, persistence, or willfulness.

Our will is a significant part of our soul. Our will can be seen as our strength of character, driving force, or motivation. Our will can cause us to be seen as persistent or stubborn, it depends on our state of mind. As stated earlier, GOD gave man a soul and made him a being with a free will. According to Merriam-Webster's dictionary, free will is defined as a voluntary choice or decision. Free will is also defined as the ability or freedom to make choices that are not determined by prior causes or by divine intervention. When GOD created man and placed him in the garden, the tree of the knowledge of good and evil was already there in the midst. Adam had access to the tree, but he had to make a choice not to eat from it. GOD knew that to Adam the tree would look good, but He did not give it to Adam for food; therefore, no matter how good the fruit of the tree looked, Adam, had to tell himself "no you can't have it." You cannot choose your race/ethnicity, but you can choose to have sex as well as choose the person that you decide to have intercourse with. Many times, we make decisions or choices based on the cravings of our carnal nature or our feelings. An old song Secret Lovers asks the question "how could something so wrong be so right?" The song goes on to say that "living two lives ain't easy at all." You see many times we try to justify what we do based on how it makes us feel (our flesh) which results in conflict in our inner man. We must choose to crucify our flesh along with its carnal desires by telling it "no, you can't have it."

Romans 8:13-14 (KJV)
For if ye live after the flesh, ye shall die: but if ye through the Spirit do mortify the deeds of the body, ye shall live. Vs 14 For as many as are led by the Spirit of God, they are the sons of God.

It is amazing that GOD allows us to choose whether to serve him or not as an act of our free will. Considering all that He has done for us, GOD wants us to love Him as an act of our will and not as an act of obligation. An individual may have multiple thoughts and desires in his/her mind at one time (will to do good or evil); however, what he/she does is based on what they desire the most (the thing that had the greatest influence on their soul). GOD wants us to desire Him more than anyone or anything else and as a result, choose to serve Him and not the desires of our carnal nature. Often times we have submitted ourselves to the desires of the flesh without realizing that we have. Some things just seem so natural. That is because they are natural; we are walking according to the desires of our human nature. The Word of GOD tells us that the urges of our natural man are antagonistic to the desires of the Holy Spirit, and the desires of the Spirit are contradictory to the urges of our carnal nature.

These opposing urges and desires are continually at war with each other. Now the actions and practices of our human nature are but not limited to the following: Adultery, fornication (sexual immorality and harlotry), impurity, total irresponsibility and lack of self-control (licentiousness), idolatry (pride), witchcraft, hatred, strife, jealousy, anger, selfishness, divisions, factions that encourage heresies, envy, murders, drunkenness, and riotous behavior (Galatians 5:19-21). All of these actions and behaviors are a part of our godless human nature or the flesh of man without the covering glory of GOD. Thanks be to God for his indescribable gift. Jesus died that we might not live after the nature of our sinful flesh but after the nature of the Spirit of GOD. The Word of GOD admonishes us to be holy for GOD is holy. This becomes a sore spot because of the word holy. Why live holy, no one else is doing it?

You see it is in our human nature to sin, but GOD does not want us to live according to our natural desires when He has a supernatural plan for our lives. Many will say no one is perfect and I will agree that all have sinned. I truly understand that the cravings and desires of our carnal nature can become so strong. Sometimes the urges and desires that come from our human existence make us feel like Pookie (New Jack City). "It be callin me man, be callin me. I just gotta go to it." Because of his inward struggle with his inward nature, the Apostle Paul stated that he was a wretched and miserable man and then he asked who will rescue and set him free from this corrupt, mortal existence (Romans 7:24)? Thanks be to GOD, those who belong to Christ Jesus have crucified the sinful nature of the flesh with its emotions, passions, appetites, and desires. We now have the ability to live a new life by the power of the Holy Spirit, but we must choose to have our conduct empowered by the Holy Spirit that we may walk with personal integrity, godly character, and moral courage (Galatian 5:24-25). In the previous sentence, one of the keywords is the word choose.

When we give our lives to GOD and accept His plan of salvation, He sets us free from the bondage of sin granting us the ability to choose freely whom we will serve. You see here it is again, free will. The desires that we experience in our flesh are real, and they are very common, but we have the freedom of choice. We must understand that every day is filled with choices. It's not about how mad they made us. It's about should we cuss them out or better yet knock them out. It's not about how they have treated us. It's about how do we choose to respond or treat them. The Bible declares that vengeance belongs to GOD, but have you ever felt like saying "GOD don't worry about it, I am going to handle this one." The carnal desires of our flesh are common and can be very strong. Because our desires and emotions are common and strong, we can be made to feel as if it's okay or feel as if we do not have a choice. Have you ever heard someone say "if this were wrong GOD would not have made me this way"?

GOD gave man the command to reproduce as well as the desire to have sex, but He also gave the institution of marriage for sex to be legal. GOD has given to everyone the measure of faith and yet He tells us not to believe everything that we hear. You see, every day it is about our choice, it is about our will. This why the Apostle Paul admonishes us to go onto maturity (perfection) because as we mature we will make better choices.

As long as we are a child, we will make childish decisions, but when we become mature, we put away childish things.

Our growth in GOD is a constant process of growing and maturing in the Word of GOD. As we grow in the Word of GOD, the way we reason, imagine, and discern begins to change ultimately resulting in a change in our actions. The Scriptures declare that in times of our ignorance and immaturity GOD winked at or overlooked and ignored our idolatry and stubbornness, but now He commands that we come to a place of maturity and repentance. Our Heavenly Father wants us to mature; no longer reasoning, imagining, and discerning as one who is irresponsible, inexperienced, or lacking knowledge. He wants us to develop our soul to a place where we feel remorse and repent for our sins (past, present, and future) and make a choice to accomplish His purpose for our lives (Acts 17:30-31).

GOD understands that our maturing in Him is a continuous process of taking off the old man and putting on the new. That's why He tells us that a righteous man may fall seven times only to rise again. If Jesus told Peter that we must forgive someone four hundred ninety times a day if they repent, how much more would our heavenly Father forgive us if we truly repent (keyword - truly repent). Does this mean that we can continue in sin? GOD forbid! What I am saying is, if we do fall, we still have a choice. We can stay there in our sin and give up because we feel as if the cravings and desires of our human nature are too strong, or we can get back up and continue to press forward in GOD asking daily for His forgiveness, His mercy, His guidance, and His grace.

Romans 7:15-25 (AMPC)
Vs15 For I do not understand my own actions [I am baffled, bewildered]. I do not practice or accomplish what I wish, but I do the very thing that I loathe [which my moral instinct condemns]. Vs16 Now if I do [habitually] what is contrary to my desire, [that means that] I acknowledge and agree that the Law is good (morally excellent) and that I take sides with it. Vs17 However, it is no longer I who do the deed, but the sin [principle] which is at home in me and has possession of me. Vs18 For I know that nothing good dwells within me, that is, in my flesh. I can will what is right, but I cannot perform it. [I have the intention and urge to do what is right, but no power to carry it out.]

There is a line in an old movie that states, "it's by will alone I set my mind in motion." Our will give us focus and determination. Our will is our driving or motivating force, and it determines how bad we want something and how far we are willing to go in order to obtain what we want. When we set our will toward something that means that we have truly made up our mind. This is why the great dragon, that old serpent, called the Devil and Satan continually tries to deceive and seduce the whole world. Satan wants to either break our will or get us to focus our inner drive and motivation on the wrong things. Jesus told Peter that Satan wanted to sift him as wheat (Luke 22:31). The act of sifting is the process of forcing material through a sieve or the process of applying pressure sufficient enough to reduce a substance to a smaller or fine particle. The Devil wanted to apply adequate pressure on Peter in an attempt to break Peter's will, causing him to lose faith and quit. That is why Jesus said, "but I have prayed for you, that your faith fails you not." We must remember that our faith is not physical activity, but mental activity that can alter our physical. Jesus did not pray that GOD would stop Satan's attack, but he prayed that the Father would strengthen Peter's resolve giving him the motivation to continue to act on his beliefs in spite of the pressure. How long can we endure and stay motivated during times of intense pressure? The trial of Job was a test of his will. Would he still trust GOD after losing everything? The Word of GOD declared that Satan, like a serpent, rose up against Israel, seducing David to count the people even though GOD told him not to number them (1Chronicles 21:1).

Have you ever experienced the loss of a loved one that shook you to your core? Many have a tough time getting up in the morning and going to work (school, etc.). This is because their will to live or move forward has been impacted. If we are not careful, we can make it seem as if that person was our sole reason for getting up in the morning or even smiling. I am the youngest of six children, and I can remember the loss of one of my brothers in 1990, my mom's only bother in 1991, and my mom's mother in 1993. That was a tough point in my life, but I never felt like giving up, and my desire to keep moving forward was strong. When my two remaining brothers died, and my mom was placed on dialysis that was an emotionally tough point, but I was motivated to keep moving. You see, I loved my brothers, but they were not my driving force. But when my mom died, I felt an emotional pain that I had never felt before. I never thought about it like this but, in my mind, she was a major reason I finished college. Few years after I graduated I made her retire. She was a major reason I worked so hard. I wanted to provide her with some of the finer things in life. When she was in the hospital for the last time, I knew that was it. Trying to appear emotionally together, I began to call my family to let them know.

On the outside I appeared strong but, on the inside, I was struggling. My will to move forward was truly being tested, and for a moment I was not sure if I could. I remember going back to work not because I was strong or feeling better, but because I was running from (avoiding) my thoughts and tears. However, even then I would still find myself in my office with eyes filled tears, and my heart feeling overwhelmed. I can remember crying out to GOD, and it was then that I realized that it was not that I could not move forward, it was a question of did I want to continue to move forward. I realized all the time that I was feeling stuck was because I made a choice. Yes, it was a struggle, but I was the one making a choice to focus my loss and not her gain. I learned that I did not have to get over or forget about my loved ones. Instead, I had to get through the emotional pain that I felt. I will always remember the love that I have for my mother but more than that I will always remember the love that she had for me. My love for her will not allow me to get over her, but GOD's love for me will help me get through the emotional hurt and pain that tries to hinder me. Because of the LORD my inner drive and motivation were strengthened, and as a result, I can choose to move forward regardless of my emotions. GOD has to be our reason why. Why we get up. Why we live. Why we love. Remember GOD wants to be our driving force. He wants to be the one that sets our will in motion.

In the gospel according to Matthew the thirteenth chapter, Jesus tells the parable of seed (the Word of GOD) being sown on different types of soil. In verse twenty Jesus describes a person who initially received the word of GOD with joy; however, because of trials and tribulations their will was broken, and they lost their drive or motivation to continue cultivating the word that was sown in their heart. Verse twenty-two Jesus describes the person that lost focus on the promises of GOD because they allowed the cares of this world and the deceitfulness of riches to become their driving or motivating force. Ask yourself, what is your motivation for doing what you do? The answer to that question will reveal who you are choosing to serve. For example, why do you read the Bible? If your answer is because you want to find the answers to your problems, your focus is on the cares of this world. What happens if you can't seem to find any answers that work the way you want them to, in the time frame that you have set? Will you continue to read? Each of us has to answer that question on our own. But, what if your answer is because you want to know GOD and understand His ways, then you are going to reap a true harvest (GOD). For he that comes to GOD must know and trust that He is and that he rewards those that seek him with constant and passionate effort (Hebrews 11:6).

The trying of our faith is really the testing of our motivating force or willpower (resolve, determination, insistence, persistence). The Bible tells us to count it all joy when we encounter various trials and tests, knowing that when our faith is being tried, it is done to develop our patience, endurance, and resolve (James 1:2-3). Romans chapter five verse three tells us that we should celebrate in the midst of our problems (trials and tribulations) knowing that these problems are used to develop our endurance and strength of character (will). Our will is what allows us to wait patiently on the promises of GOD. Jesus declared that we should love the LORD our GOD with all of our heart, soul, mind, and strength (Luke 10:27). Jesus is admonishing us to love the LORD our GOD with every aspect of our inner man. We have to choose or will ourselves to love GOD in this way. Your will is a powerful aspect of your soul. Your will allows you to follow GOD even when it seems like everyone else is doing their own thing. Your will can also lead you to go against the advice of others and even against the desires of GOD. Your will plays a major role in influencing your choices. GOD wants us to focus our driving force on Him and His ways. Our will to please and serve GOD must be stronger than our will to please our flesh. Another way to say this is, pleasing GOD and doing His will must be our driving force. Serving the LORD must be the thing that sets our mind in motion. We give to those in need not for the praise of man but to the glory of GOD. Whatever we do we must do it as unto the LORD.

Colossians 3:23 (AMPC)
Whatever may be your task, work at it heartily (from the soul), as [something done] for the Lord and not for men, Vs 24 Knowing [with all certainty] that it is from the Lord [and not from men] that you will receive the inheritance which is your [real] reward. [The One Whom] you are actually serving [is] the Lord Christ (the Messiah).

In the soul, we have the ability to follow whomever we choose. And whomever you choose to serve/obey becomes your master (Romans 6:16). The word master is merely the ultimate authority. Let me explain if you have multiple job offers; however, you chose to come work for me. You do not have to call me master, you do not have to say yes sir or no sir; however, I am still the ultimate authority. Because I can control what time you come to work, what time you leave work, how you dress for work, how to complete your work, I cannot tell you what to eat, but I can control how long it takes for you to eat. So, you may not call me master because I pay you but as long as you are on the job you serve me, and I am in control (that's not a great work environment, but it is true). Now you have a choice, you can quit or not. If you want to quit, but you feel as if you cannot, the question becomes why not? I am sure many slaves wanted to quit, but they felt like they could not because they felt as if they did not have enough power. It appeared as if they were not in control. But then you had those that said enough is enough. They did not only want to be free, but their desire to be free was so strong that it caused them to move regardless of the potential outcomes. Many blacks had to move to the back of the bus or give up their seat for their white counterparts. I am sure many of them wanted to sit at the front of the bus or just keep their seat. But their wants did not make them sit or stay seated; however, when their will was stirred from the inside, it gave them the passion and boldness to sit when others were afraid to stand. Often times we stand up for what is right not just because it is right but because we have truly gotten tired of sitting down. Did Rosa Parks stay seated because she wanted to be known for starting a movement or was it because on that day she was tired and enough was enough? I am not saying that she was physically exhausted, but she had grown tired of the injustices, and she made up her mind (set her will) that enough is enough. It is during times of adversity do we see what is really on the inside of us. It is during the rough times in life we get a chance to see the strength of our character and our driving force. It is during these times our will (resolve) is either strengthened or it is broken.

Who have you submitted your will too? Many times, we remain submitted to something or someone because we have not truly made up our mind to leave. We have not set our wills in motion. If we stay somewhere when down on the inside we want to leave many times it is because we feel trapped and we lack the motivation or the courage to leave. Have you ever seen someone that was considered strong-willed or stubborn? These individuals appear to be courageous or crazy because they would always do things that they were told not to do regardless of the consequences. You see it is a matter of your will (motivation, driving force). You can be free if you want to. You can be successful if you want to. You can stay married if you want to. The question is how bad do you want to be free, successful, or married? Is the driving force within you strong enough do what is necessary? Our driving force allows us to make choices based on desire and not right or wrong.

Ask yourself, how many laws would you break to save your child or a loved one's life? When faced with this situation most people would not be thinking about what is right or wrong. Most would be focusing on one overriding objective, and that is saving a life. You see our internal drive when ignited by emotions will cause us to make choices that disregard all potentially negative outcomes as it continues to move us toward one singular goal. Question? Have you ever felt like if you did not get something that you thought was necessary you were going to die? If I don't get my coffee, I am going to die. If I don't get some sex, I am going to die. Because our minds, if functioning properly, are hard-wired to preserve life and as a result we subconsciously make choices focusing on one overruling objective, and that objective is whatever is deemed necessary to preserve life.

What if you are working in a company that pays you well, and you like what you are doing, but the company does a lot of unscrupulous things? Why don't you quit? Is it because you have grown accustomed to a particular way of living? How many of you would probably want to leave your job but the bills said you better stay; how are you going to take care of us if you quit? Often times, we can find ourselves in a place of hopelessness having our willpower broken. We have the desire to leave, but there is the will stay, to maintain our current lifestyle. This level of double-mindedness causes distress in our mind which can have a negative effect on our body. To relieve the stress, we do that which seems easiest. Many of us say we want the freedom to choose, but in actuality true choice creates a dilemma and dilemmas create stress and stress can lead to death. Therefore, we often say to the LORD, do not give me a choice, just make it clear. What job am I supposed to take? Just make it clear. Whom am I to marry? Just make it clear. Is Jesus the way to salvation and should I give my life to him? GOD, just make it clear. We want GOD to move all of life's choices out of our way and leave us with the only option. The Scriptures calls for us to be holy because GOD is holy. But now we say, GOD, there must be another way. When it comes to loving, serving, and living for Him, we want multiple options. The Bible declares that if we love GOD, we should keep his laws and be consistently mindful of His precepts and teachings. The Scripture further declares that we should not consider the laws, precepts, and teachings of the LORD burdensome, oppressive, or grievous (1John 5:3). However, often times, when we are trying to live for Him we place unfair expectations on ourselves when we are mere babes or immature ones in Christ. These unrealistic expectations that we place on ourselves can cause us to feel stressed, and as a result, our motivation fades away leaving us with a feeling of hopelessness and depression. We must learn to receive GOD's help through His Word and His Spirit. I can remember when I got baptized with water how I was moved with emotion and gratitude for all that Christ has done for me. However, when I came out of the water, the only thing that was different about me was the fact that I and my clothes were soaking wet. There was nothing different about my carnal man and the way I thought. I understand that what the book of Romans chapter six says concerning being baptized into his death and being resurrected in the newness of life. But, it was not until I grew in the Word and Spirit of GOD that a noticeable change truly occurred. By the power of the Spirit and Word of GOD, we can be rescued from our bodies that have been infected with sin (Romans 7:24). We must understand that we cannot live for the Father in our own strength. That is Jesus said that he would not leave us comfortless, but he would send us another comforter, and he will be with and dwell in us because when it comes down to it; we do not have multiple options but just one choice. JESUS! He is the way, the truth, and the life. Jesus is the only way to receive eternal salvation and if anyone tries to come to GOD any other way they are considered a thief and a robber. There are some good people in this world, but as stated earlier just because something (someone) is good does not mean that it is GOD.

THE HELMET OF SALVATION

In the world of American football, equipment is so important. With the incidence of head injuries like concussions and chronic traumatic encephalopathy (CTE), nothing is more important than the helmet. I can remember when I was in sixth grade playing Pop Warner football, I did not have cleats, so I wore a pair of orange Converse All-Stars. I was allowed to participate without cleats, but they would not allow me to play without my helmet. Cleats are important, but not as important as the helmet. In some construction areas, individuals are not permitted to enter without a hard hat. This is also true when placed in a combat zone, as a part of the standard equipment, everyone is issued a helmet. The helmet is designed to protect an individual's head from shrapnel and ballistic threats. The Bible declares though we are made of flesh, our war is not against the flesh, and the weapons of our warfare are not carnal; therefore, we must put on the full armor of GOD in order to stand and resist the strategies of the devil. The Scriptures tells us above all take the shield of faith, the helmet of salvation and the sword of the Spirit. Even in GOD's army or on His team the helmet is vitally important.

The word "salvation" which is used in various Scriptures throughout the Bible has many definitions. The following is a list of definitions used to define our American English word "salvation."

- Deliverance or preservation from material and temporal danger and apprehension.
- Spiritual and eternal deliverance.
- Deliverance, it is the aspect that brings you out of bondage, sickness, and death, brought on by sin.

The major word in the New Testament for "salvation" is the Greek word "Soteria" (reference # G4991), which can mean to deliver, salvation, save, saving, and health. Another word used in the New Testament for salvation is the Greek word "soterion" (reference # G4992). This word is only seen in approximately five Scriptures, and it means salvation, defender, or defense (by implication). The Bible tells us to put on the helmet of salvation (Ephesians 6:17). The Greek word here for salvation is "soterion." If we were to take another look at this passage of Scripture, we would see that the Apostle Paul began listing tools that are used to protect the believer in a battle with or an attack from the enemy. This may explain why the apostle chose to use the Greek word "soterion" instead of the Greek word "Soteria." Apostle Paul is telling us to put on the helmet of defense or the helmet of salvation as a defense against an enemy that lies in wait. To lie in wait is the act of concealing yourself to attack by surprise. Lie in wait also means to hide and wait for the right moment to make an attack. One of Satan's strategies against the believer is the art of surprise. Satan likes to attack us in areas of our lives where we are weakest or when we are not focused.

Romans 13:11 (KJV)
And that, knowing the time, that now it is high time to awake out of sleep: for now is our salvation nearer than when we believed.

The enemy of our soul wants us to have a false sense of security and think more highly of ourselves than we ought to think. As a result, we fall asleep when we should be watching and praying. As stated earlier, Jesus warned Peter that Satan desired to sift him (Peter) as wheat; however, Peter was unsuspecting of the enemy's plan. Peter was overconfident in his own abilities. Peter's response to Christ was all men shall be enticed to sin or fall away because of you, but I will never be enticed to sin, I am ready to go with you to prison and to death. If we continue to read through the gospel of Matthew chapter twenty-six, we will find Peter sleeping when he should have been watching and praying that he does not fall or enter into temptation. Peter's failure to prepare for battle was not physical, but mental. Often times, Satan attacks our mind, will, and emotions. He desires for us to become weakened mentally to the point that we lose faith, and without faith, it is impossible to please GOD (Hebrew 11:6). Most of the biggest challenges that we face are mental and spiritual that manifest in the natural.

Although we are in the flesh, we do not fight a war with our flesh because our greatest weapons are not made of this world, but they are from GOD. We do not fight against natural forces made of flesh and blood, but our true battle is against principalities, against powers, against the rulers of the darkness of this world, and against spiritual wickedness in high places. The Word of GOD declares, the weapons of our warfare are not carnal, but they are mighty through GOD to the pulling down of strongholds, casting down imaginations, reasoning (carnal and fleshly ways of thinking) as well as every proud and vain thought that exalts itself against the knowledge of GOD (2Corinthians 10:3-5 and Ephesians 6:10-12). A stronghold may be defined as a fortified place; a place of security or survival; or a mindset (way of thinking, state of mind, attitude, or an outlook) that an individual has that accepts things as unchangeable or necessary for security and survival. To breakdown, pull down and destroy these strongholds/mindsets, we must genuinely understand GOD's word concerning our salvation that we may be truly saved or delivered. The enemy will use any trick and use anyone he can to cause Christians to stop short of GOD's plan for their eternal salvation or to lose faith in GOD's plan of salvation; either way, you will not receive GOD's salvation. Satan tries to set up strongholds in the minds of people, in order to deceive them and lead them astray.

In Peter's mind, he was stronger than he actually was. The Bible would consider Peter as acting presumptuously. Peter was fully aware of what he was doing, and he had knowledge about the risk that was associated with his actions and yet he deliberately set his mind to do it. It was as if he wanted to show or prove to Jesus how faithful and brave he was. The Apostle Paul warns us to be careful and not to think of yourselves more highly than you ought to think. This weakness was always present in Peter; however, Peter saw it as strength. Often times when a person fails or does not succeed in something that they were very confident or sure that they would succeed in, they lose faith. In many cases, they begin to question everyone and everything, and for many, this leads to depression. This is why Jesus prayed that Peter's faith did not fail. I have seen so many students who have graduated from high school never making anything less than an "A." However, if the same student makes a grade of "C" or worse they fail a course while in college, they would spiral downward. This is also true of many believers. Have you ever believed that GOD was going to do something? I mean you just knew it because he has always done it in the past; therefore, you begin to take actions based on what you believed GOD for. How did you feel when it didn't happen? When you prayed for someone to live, and they died. You prayed for things to get better and things seemed to get worse. In times like these, many of us would say we still believe GOD; however, in our heart we have questions. These questions can cause us to become emotionally compromised. We understand that our faith is not based on physical strength, but inner power. When our inner man is emotionally weakened, we begin to ask questions. We begin to ask "GOD, if you love me" or "GOD, do you hear me"?

THE HELMET OF SALVATION

2 Corinthians 2:11 (KJV)
Lest Satan should get an advantage of us: for we are not ignorant of his devices.

The Bible tells us that when the expectation is delayed, it makes our heart (mind) sick (Proverbs 13:12). Most people do not have the stamina (endurance, resilience, determination) to fight a good fight when they are ill/weak (mentally). Remember our enemy (Satan) likes to attack us in areas of our lives where we are weakest or where we are not focused. Matthew the fourth chapter verses two and three declared Satan waited until Jesus was hungry before he tempted him. He tempted Christ saying "if you are the son of GOD command these stones to be made into loaves of bread." Hungry simply means to have an appetite, a strong desire or a craving for something. We can become hungry for a lot of things, i.e., food, excitement, friendship, and sex, just to name a few. When we are really hungry for something that is right in front of us, it is at that point when we truly come face to face with temptation. Our spirit man may be saying no, but our flesh is screaming YES! Satan lies in wait, concealing himself waiting for the right moment to make an attack. In moments when we are hungry, frustrated, disappointed, or even upset with GOD our faith is at its weakest point, and in moments like these Satan is waiting to pounce. That is why Apostle Paul told us to put on the helmet of salvation as a defense against an enemy that lies in wait. The apostle Paul also said, "I have fought a good fight; I have finished my course; I have kept the faith (2 Timothy 4:7). This passage of scripture as well as others seems

177

to imply that the enemy (Satan, The Devil) wants to discourage us, pressure us, oppress us and so on; ultimately wanting to cause us to lose faith in or doubt GOD and His Son Jesus Christ. One of the tools or weapons of defense that the LORD has given us to protect ourselves against the attack of the Devil is the helmet of salvation or the helmet of defense. The enemy fights us a majority of the time in our minds. The Bible says that we are to be transformed (changed in character or condition; converted) by the renewing of our minds (Romans 12:2).

GUARD YOUR EMOTIONS

In the words of a broken heart
It's just emotion that's taken me over
Tied up in sorrow, lost in my soul
Bee Gees "Emotion"

A s beings that have a soul, we must understand that our
emotional makeup is an important part of who we are.
When Jesus was asked, which is the preeminent and
most important commandment of all? He answered saying,
"The first and most important is: Hear, O Israel, the LORD our
GOD is one Lord. You must love Him with all of your thoughts
and feelings, with your life, which animates the body, and with
all of your mental faculties and imagination, and with all of
your abilities, might, and power: this is the first
commandment. And the second commandment is like it,
namely this; you must unselfishly love your neighbor as
yourself. These are the most important, and there are no other
commandments greater than these" (Mark 12:30-31). To keep
these commandments, we must engage our emotions and not
rely on pure logic. The Scriptures declare that the just should
live by their faith, and the righteous should walk by faith and
not by sight. We must learn how to think logically, and at the

same time, we cannot allow ourselves to be confined by the limitations that our human reasoning may create. True passion motivates us to go beyond restrictions created by what we would call common-sense. When we comprehend this, we will understand that when we teach the law, we are teaching in a sense logic, which gives us structure as well as creates boundaries. Logic says, "If this, then that." However, as Disciples of Christ, we are taught to instill passion (love and affection). The Word of GOD declares, for the joy that was set before him, Christ endured the cross and ignored the shame. That was not logical love but a kind love that is motivated by a heart full of concentrated and guided emotion.

The word emotions can be defined as an instinctive state of mind that is the byproduct of a person's environment, mood, or relationships. Merriam Webster further defines emotions as a conscious mental reaction that is subjectively experienced as a strong feeling and is usually directed toward a specific object and is often accompanied by physiological and behavioral changes. Often times we are consciously aware of how we are feeling toward someone or something; however, we are not necessarily in control of how we respond or react. The word "Emotion" is derived from a Latin word that means to stir up, remove, or displace; hence to disturb. As I began to define the word, "emotion" thoughts began to flood my mind of how our emotions have the ability to push us to do or say things that we normally would not do or say. Emotions, also known as our feelings, affections, passions, or sentiments, can alter our attitudes or our established ways of thinking about someone or something (typical tendencies) and move us from our normal baseline to a heightened or suppressed demonstrative state. Our emotions are a powerful influence on our behavior, and if we are not careful when we become overly emotional, we lose our ability to choose our actions. We can be consciously aware of how we feel and yet our reactions can be so instinctive that we appear to be in an unintentional or almost unconscious state. We must learn to pause and respond based on our inner principles, not our emotions or outside influences. When our feelings are getting the best of us our behavior becomes reactive; thus, we are allowing outside influences to dictate how we respond. We start saying things like, "they made me" or "I couldn't help it." You see these statements imply that we are not in control.

Question, if you are not in control of you, who is? We must remain conscious of our actions as well as our feelings. Premeditated or calculated behavior gives us the freedom to choose our response based on our principles or desired results and not our feelings. Our freedom to choose expands as we allow for space between the emotional trigger and our response. Knowing and understanding the emotional triggers that angers, embarrasses, motivates, frustrates, and inspires us is vital to our overall growth and spiritual maturity. When we learn to observe ourselves objectively, in difficult situations, we are able to recognize and manage our emotions (especially negative ones) that are at work in us. This recognition gives us the opportunity to pause avoiding an impulsive reaction, giving us the ability to think clearly and impartially. As a result; we can act according to GOD's purpose and not our passions. Have you ever played a game of chess, poker, or even pool? If so, you would notice that some people react and some like to take their time and reason. The person that reacts is acting only off of their emotions based on what is in front of them or what is currently vibrating in their mind right now, as well as what has already occurred. They are left feeling as if there is no other choice. On the other hand, a player who reasons thinks of past, present, and future options. This person sees different choices. In the game of life, this is how it is with us daily. We either spend our life reacting as if there is only one choice, or we spend our life reasoning looking at all the possibilities.

In the book of Proverbs, the fourth chapter verse twenty-three tells us to protect or guard our heart with all diligence because out of it flows the results and outcomes of life. The Hebrew word for heart in that passage of Scripture is widely used for the feelings, the will, and the intellect. King David said to himself that he would keep watch over his tongue to keep from sinning. He stated that he tried to muzzle his mouth while he was in the presence of wicked people. The King stated. "I said nothing, not even something good, and my distress deepened. As I thought about it, my heart (feelings) within me became more and more enraged, and then I spoke" (Psalms 39:1-3). You see his emotions got the best of him. They stirred him up or created such a disturbance in his inner man that he could no longer contain himself. Have you ever been so angry that you said or did something that you know you should not have said or done? Reacting impulsively based on intense emotions often leaves us with feelings of regret and shame. Our passions also can give others the idea that we are courageous or bold. Question, if you tell your boss how you really feel about them or the job, are you blunt or were you just emotional? Boldness does not require anger or any other type of emotion to cause us to move. Some of you may say that you would have said something before, but you did not want to hurt their feelings, "but they made me so mad." So, your emotional state caused you to hurt someone intentionally when other times you would not because you know that it would be wrong. The Word of GOD tells us to be angry but sin not (Ephesians 4:26). Hmmm! Our emotional state can allow us to tap into a source of internal power, or it can destroy our will and lead to inner weakness and depression. Our Passions can be a source of positive or negative energy; therefore, guard your heart with all diligence. When King David and his men saw their city burned with fire and their families taken captive, the Bible declares that some of the men wept so much so that they had no more power or strength within them to weep. The Scriptures states two hundred of the men who were with David were so overcome with emotion, they were faint (emotionally and physically fatigued). They were so exhausted that they could not go over the brook Besor and fight for what was theirs (1Samuel 30: 3-6). I do not know about you, but I have been there. I think most of us have felt like that at some point in our lives. For me, there have been times throughout my life where I was so overcome with emotion that I did not have the strength nor the desire to fight. Smiling on the outside, while

183

totally distraught on the inside. Many pastors/clergy experience the severe emotional highs and lows of ministry. Data shows that when it comes to suicides, ministry can be dangerous work. The Scriptures advises us in the third chapter of the book of James that many of us should not become teachers, because those that teach are judged more critically than others and are more severely condemned. The Scripture goes on to say that we all make mistakes and often stumble as well as we offend others; as a result, this emotional roller coaster called pastoring ends in suicide for many (James 3:1-2). In the movie Spiderman, Norman Osborn stated that the cunning warrior does not attack the mind nor the body but matters of the heart (emotions). If a person can break your heart, they will ultimately break your spirit and wear down your body.

Understanding all aspects of salvation is a powerful tool to keep our emotions in check (see chapter – "Helmet of Salvation"). If we confess our sins, He is faithful and just to forgive us of our sins, and He is more than able to cleanse of our unrighteousness. As a result, when our heart tries to condemn us we will know without a shadow of a doubt that GOD is greater than our hearts. As believers, we all must understand the three tenses of salvation. We are saved; we are being saved, and we shall be saved. We are saved through justification, and as a result, we are set free from the bondage and guilt of sin. We are being saved through the process of sanctification; therefore, we are being freed from the power and influence of sin. In Philippians the first chapter, the

Apostle Paul was persuaded and sure of the fact that He that has begun a good work in us will continue working until the day of Jesus Christ. He will continue to work on developing, perfecting, and bringing that good work in us to full completion right up to the time of his return. We shall be saved through the process of glorification no longer living in the presence of sin because we shall be with him and like him. The Scriptures declare that we must wait patiently and eagerly for the redemption and transformation of our bodies at the resurrection where our adoption as sons will be complete (Romans 6 – Romans 8).

Not only can the highs and lows of trying to live a sanctified life have the ability to make us emotional, but the Bible also tells us that delayed/overdue hope can make us emotionally sick as well. Have you ever said, "I want everything that GOD has promised me, but I am too tired"? Be not weary in well-doing, for in due season, we shall reap if we do not give up and quit. Has someone quoted that scripture to you, or you have read it and thought to yourself "I know but when is my season?" Have you ever said, "I don't know how much more I can take, or I don't know how much longer I can wait?" Question? Are you tired or emotional? Often times if we can get our emotions under control, we somehow find the strength to continue to pursue after the promises of GOD. When we get our feelings out of the way, we find out that we have some more inner strength, and we can go further and handle more than we thought. When we are living based on our feelings, we become impatient.

We must learn to wait patiently for the promises of GOD. The testing of our faith through life experiences produces a mental fortitude that leads to spiritual maturity and inner peace that allows us to move forward in hope. In sports, the emotions of the crowd can stir and push their team to victory. However, it is not uncommon for a team to feel drained and struggle after an emotional victory or defeat. Emotions can be seen as the difference between torque and horsepower in a car. When we think of torque as it is related to a car, we think of the force required to get a vehicle moving from a state of motion to another (acceleration). Torque also is seen as the vehicle's ability to pull. While horsepower (relative to weight) is a better measure of your vehicle's highest possible speed, the energy required to move a vehicle for standing still to sixty miles per hour rapidly is much more than necessary to keep it there once in motion. Hence in the city, you burn more gas because you are constantly stopping and starting, going from zero to sixty. Like torque, our emotions are great to get us started or pull us out a rut, but living off of our emotions daily can leave us drained.

How we feel can skew our outlook on life. When we are happy life is good, and GOD is good. However, when we are frustrated, angry, sorrowful, etc. life is terrible, and we begin to ask questions (Proverbs 15:13 and 17:22). GOD, where are you? LORD, do you love me? Our sentiments can be the enemy of true justice. Emotions can cause us to condemn quickly and speak curses over the lives of those that have hurt us (hurt our heart), including ourselves. Our emotions can make it difficult for us to forgive those who have trespassed against us. Those same emotions will cause us to stay with someone knowing that we should leave. Our passions can overwhelm or overpower our ability to think and reason, thus causing us to do what we would not ordinarily (logically) do. A guy who is known as a good person that would not hurt anyone, and yet he is in prison for murder. Why? He walks in on his wife having an affair with his friend. The sensations of hurt, betrayal, jealousy, anger all run through his mind. If these emotions are able to overpower his logic or ability to reason, he will either react in a violent rage (hence he is locked up), or his mind will go into complete shutdown.

Have you ever heard someone say that they were so mad that they could not talk? When we are able to reason within ourselves, we are suggesting that there are multiple options; thus we have a conference within our minds trying to decide which option is best for us. However, if our emotions overtake us, we will not think or reason rationally we will just react based on the feelings that were the strongest in our disturbed state. There are so many people incarcerated because they felt as if they had no other choice or simply put, they reacted based on their emotions (in the heat of the moment). A crime of passion usually denotes to a violent crime, in which the wrongdoer commits an act against someone because of a sudden strong impulse. Impulse power may be a good thing in space travel (Star Trek) but living off of impulse can be dangerous in our personal lives.

Just like a husband is jealous about his wife, the Bible tells us that GOD is a jealous GOD, and He is jealous concerning us. The Bible tells us that GOD will not share His glory with anyone because He is a jealous GOD. The Apostle Paul said in his second letter to the church at Corinth "I am jealous over you with godly jealousy: for I have espoused you to one husband that I may present you as a chaste virgin to Christ" (2Corinthians 11:2). Joshua admonished the people not to forsake the LORD, by serving strange gods. Joshua reminded them that GOD is a jealous GOD (Joshua 24:19-20). The LORD is full of emotions as are we. However, unlike man in his carnal state, the LORD can control His emotions. The Scriptures declare that GOD is slow to anger and plenteous in mercy, and His mercies towards us are new every morning. GOD loves us so much that He becomes jealous when we give our love, praise, and worship to someone or something else. GOD's love for us is not only moral and just; it is active and full of emotion. Think about it. It does not make logical sense for Christ to give himself for us while we were yet in our sins and enemies with GOD, but he died for us anyway. Romans the fifth chapter verse eight declares that GOD clearly demonstrated and proved His love for us. Because while we were still considered sinners in His eyes, GOD sent Christ to die for us. The Word of GOD declares for the joy that was set before Christ, he suffered on the cross and ignored the shame. Now that is love; moral, righteous, unconditional, and emotional love. When our emotions are stirred, they can bring out the best and worst in us. Often we hear that Christ was moved with compassion, and as a result, he fed, healed, and delivered the people. We are challenged to have our emotions moved daily to the point that we make a difference in the lives of others, but not to the point that we wear our feelings on our sleeves. When we progressively begin to recognize and understand the nature of GOD's love, we should love others the same way not in mere words but in daily practice with all sincerity. As Christ has demonstrated his compassion towards us by laying down His life for us, we should be moved with compassion and sacrifice when necessary to help others (1John 3: 16-18).

Living by our emotions is very dangerous because we begin to perform actions without conscious thought. Remember, it is possible to be aware of how we are feeling, and yet we are unaware of our actions. Our heightened emotional state causes our outward behavior to respond as if it is on autopilot. I am hired by thirty-five-year-old wife and mother as her personal trainer. As part of her training, I ask her to lift a car. She would probably look at me as if I am crazy and say, "I can't lift this car." But what if a car falls on her husband or her child. She will not hesitate, but will automatically attempt to lift the vehicle. This is because of the flood of emotions that begin to fuel her. I can remember years ago my wife, and I was riding down the highway with our two children. While I was driving, an SUV in front of us started swerving, and then it flipped over approximately three times, landed on its wheels and started rolling backward toward a body of water that was known to have alligators. When I saw this, I immediately pulled over and jumped out of my car. I was moving off of impulse power (my emotions), and I was moving without thinking about alligators. While I was jumping out of the car, I yelled to my wife "call 911!" Thankfully, she yelled back "please put the car in park!" I realized that I was not thinking, I was just reacting. Some people might say that I was thinking so much about the people in the other car that I forgot to come to a complete stop and put my car in park. Question, if I was really using my conscious mind, would I have put my entire family in danger trying to save someone whom I do not know. That is why our passion can be a powerful gift or great flaw. Our passion is what makes so many people attempt to do things that others may call heroic. I believe that this is one of the things that make this country so great, in spite of all of its flaws. You can always find someone who is willing to put their lives in danger without hesitation to save or help someone else. You can consistently find someone that has been moved with compassion. So many individuals become law enforcement officers and firefighters because they want to help others. It takes more than mere want, for a person to go into a burning building. It takes inner torque, a push of emotions or courage. Remember, it is easy to say what you would do, but true action is demonstrated in the heat of the moment. I have heard of people fighting off a shark to save a stranger, people jumping into a body of water to save a family from a sinking vehicle and more. Being fueled by our emotions can be a powerful motivator; however, constantly living off of them can be a terrible flaw.

WHAT DO YOU VALUE?

John 15:19 (KJV)
If ye were of the world, the world would love his own: but because ye are not
of the world, but I have chosen you out of the world, therefore the world
hateth you.

As believers, we must understand that we are in this world, but we are no longer of this world; therefore, we must be careful not to fall in love with this world and the things that are associated with it (1John 2:15). For example, money is not evil; however, the love of money is considered to be the root of all evil (1Timothy 6:10). The book of Proverbs the twenty-three chapter verse four tells us not to weary ourselves trying to become rich and to stop trusting in our own wisdom because the riches and wisdom of this world will soon fade away. You see; no man can truly serve GOD and at the same time have an excessive or greedy desire for worldly wealth or gain. The things that we value (high importance, true wealth) are usually kept in the same place in which we store our hearts. How much we truly value something is determined from within. It is essential that we recognize that the seller sets that price. However, it is the buyer that determines its true worth. I learned a long time ago if you want to increase your wealth do not seek to become rich, seek to become more valuable. People will not pay you based on your desire to be rich, but they will pay your asking price if they deem you valuable to them. Therefore, become a person of value and know your worth, but also know your market. I could price a car at a million dollars, but if no one wants to buy it, they are telling me that it is not worth that asking price. Have you ever seen something that cost what you thought was a lot of money, and you said I cannot see myself paying that much money for that/those_____ (you fill in the blank)? However, others that are in the same financial situation as you are willing to purchase the item that you would not at its current price. It is not a matter of can we afford but rather what we value. There are individuals who daily buy things that they cannot afford because something in their soul is telling them that they got to have it. There are patients who have to choose between purchasing their medications and buying groceries. Whichever they choose is determined by importance and importance is determined what we value. Remember, in our soul, we define how valuable something is to us. The more precious a thing is to us, the more we are willing to pay. Please understand payment is not always in the form of money. If the value that we have set in our inner man does not match the level of the asking price, we would say, "it is not worth it." Thanks be to GOD; He considered us valued at the asking price. He did not negotiate as to say I want to save them, but you are asking for too much. Without hesitation, at just the right time, He sent Jesus to be the propitiating and compensating sacrifice for our sins. GOD loved and valued us so much so that He gave His only begotten

Son to be the ransom for our souls. He paid the full cost of our salvation. I know some of you may be saying, Jesus tried to negotiate because he did not want to pay the full asking price saying, "Father, if there be any other way let this cup pass from me." We must remember that Jesus was GOD and man. The Spirit (GOD) is willing, but the Flesh (man) is weak. The Spirit within Jesus or the Christ in Jesus gave him the power to overcome the weakness of his flesh. Furthermore, Jesus valued pleasing his Father even if it cost him his life. Therefore, He said, "Not my will, but your will be done."

So many times in relationships value setting becomes a major problem. One spouse values things that are totally different from the other. One spouse may value family, and the other may value their freedom. It is not uncommon for one spouse to value spending time together as a family and the other may value supporting and buying things for the family. Spending time and supporting the family are both important; however, if you value supporting the family more than spending time with the family, you may find yourself always away from the family. As men, we are taught to be providers for our families, but we are not taught that in order to be a good husband and father we must spend time. I have heard this statement so many times "my dad was in the house, but he was not there." Because of how we have been taught we place more importance on our jobs and what we can provide than we do on whom we are working to provide for. This is also seen in single mothers working so hard to provide for their families that the children often times grow up on their own. One mother was frustrated because her son kept getting into trouble, so she asked him "What is your problem? I work hard, I even work extra hours to make sure you have everything that you wanted so you would not feel less than any of your friends." The child answered his mother and said, "You are the problem. You worked all the time, and you never gave me what I needed most. YOU!" See the mother valued providing, and her heart was in the place of provision; however, she was not on the same page in terms of what the child valued. As a result; she forgot to be there. In our limited thinking, it can get very confusing. It would be easy for us to sit here in think, what child does not want a new Play Station/Xbox or the latest pair of Jordan's. Yes, those things may make a child happy for a moment, but that is only temporary.

In our natural mindset, we frequently esteem providing wants/desires. As a result, we oftentimes diminish the value of meeting basic human needs. We feel a sense of pride when we are able to get our child a pair of sneakers that they really wanted. It makes us feel good on the inside to know that we worked hard to get them what they wanted and to see that excitement in their faces. We often times forget how excited our child gets when they know that we are at their game. Thinking back to when I was playing Pop Warner football, I did not always have cleats, but I knew my mother and the rest of my family was going to be there. One of my most memorable moments was not when a made a touchdown, but it was when I heard my uncle yelling with excitement "that's my nephew, that's my nephew. I can tell by the orange All-Stars." Would I have loved to have some new cleats? You better know it. However, honestly to know that they loved me so much that they would take time out of their day to come to watch me play was so much more valuable than any pair cleats money could buy.

I apologize, but I think this is a good time for me to tell my entire family, THANK YOU! Thank you for seeing the value in me and for supporting me.

Remember wherever your wealth (what you value) is stored there your heart will be as well. My family being at my game let me know that they valued me; therefore, their heart was with me. I knew that I was loved. Let me ask you a question, have you ever felt like GOD did not love you? If we are honest with ourselves, most of us will answer yes. At times, we may question GOD's love because He did not give us what we felt like we needed or wanted. However, most times we questioned GOD's love for us when it seems like He is not there. With all that Jesus suffered, he never cried out; nevertheless, when GOD removed His presence, Jesus cried out and asked, "My GOD why have you forsaken me?" GOD placed the sins of the world (past, present, and future sins) on Jesus that we might be set free from the bondage and penalty of sin. He was nailed to a tree that we might be freed from the curse. Christ became sin for us that we might become the righteousness of GOD. And because of the works of Christ and our faith in him, the Father has promised that He would never leave us nor forsake us.

In order to understand GOD's love, and how much He truly values us, we must think totally different. Even our use of the word "love" is based on worldly thinking, and it does not go beyond our natural wisdom. GOD's love extends beyond our senses, and many times it does not appear logical. It may make sense to love those that love you, but GOD's love extends to those that have turned their back on him. It may make sense to sacrifice for a person we considered godly or innocent but Christ died for those He knew were ungodly and guilty. Many of us would not give our child for a family member that we are very close to, but GOD gave his only-begotten Son for people that were considered adulterers, fornicators, liars, murderers, unbelievers, and such like. Now, in our natural minds, this does not make sense. For many people, this why salvation is so hard to believe. Why would a holy and righteous GOD sacrifice His son for us and all we have to do is believe and repent? This does not compute. Thanks be to GOD that His ways are not our ways, and His thoughts are not our thoughts. If we are going to love and please GOD, we must think differently. By the power of the Spirit of GOD, our thinking must change, and we must understand GOD from a spiritual view and not a natural or humanistic point of view. The Apostle Paul tells us, he is not speaking words that man's wisdom will teach, but he is speaking things which were imparted to him by the Holy Spirit. Through the teachings of the Holy Spirit, he is now able to compare spiritual with spiritual even though his natural man does not understand (1Corinthians 2:13-14). Our thoughts and ways must transcend our human attitudes and behaviors.

TRANSCEND

often ask, what is success? Most will say it is the accomplishment of one's goals or becoming famous. So, why is it that when we get the degree or the career that we dreamed of, some of us are still unhappy, or we don't feel successful? Some will say that success is achieving a place of happiness. The problem with that definition is that happiness comes and goes because happiness is based upon the situation that is occurring at that moment. Simply put, happiness is dependent on the happening. Therefore, based on our carnal mindset a person will never achieve ultimate success because, in this life, there will always be a time to cry (Ecclesiastes 3:1–8). In today's society, how many people do we consider successful or famous that seem to be unhappy? It is amazing how many marriages end in divorce because of money, and yet we see people with money having their marriages end in divorce as well. One of the problems is that we set goals for our career, personal life, marriage, etc., based on what we think we need or what we think we want. However, what we need or want may change. If we honestly told the truth in most situations, we do not know what we really want or need. We base everything we need or want on our here and now. Even though we make plans for our future, these plans are based on our current mindset and are liable to change. How can we reach true success if our goals are always prone to change?

To reach authentic success, we must be able to transcend (go beyond) time and see our end and our middle from the beginning. The word "transcendent" means to exceed usual limits or extend beyond the limits of ordinary experiences. Therefore, our future plans will be based on our future and not our present. By faith, we have seen the end, and we understand the process that is required in the middle; thus, our plans for success should not change once we begin. GOD declares that He is the only one that knows what will happen at the end from the beginning, and His plans will come to pass. One of the things that I love about GOD is that He thinks about me, and He has a plan for my life. Not only does He think about me; He thinks about you as well, and He has a plan for your life. I do not know what you are going through or where you are in your life, but I do know that GOD has a plan, and it will come to pass, if we keep the faith and patiently wait for it. The thoughts and plans that GOD has for us are of peace and prosperity, they are to give us hope and a future. Some of you may be asking where are the promises of GOD and when are they going to manifest. I say to you, be patient and remember that GOD is not a man that he should lie, if He said it, He is more than able to perform. The Bible declares that in the last days, there shall be those who will ridicule our faith, walking after their own desires. Saying, where is the promise of his coming? Since our fathers have died, things continue as they were from the beginning. Nothing seems to have changed. Because of this, they choose to be ignorant of the fact that by the Word of GOD, the heavens and earth were framed. And everything that exists now will be kept in store by the same word. Please do not be ignorant of this one thing, that one day with the Lord is as a thousand years and a thousand years as one day. GOD is not late concerning his promises, as some people would count tardiness; but He is actually patiently waiting on us because He does not want any of us to perish. He wants us all to come to repentance (2Peter 3:3-9).

Isaiah 46:10 (KJV)
Declaring the end from the beginning, and from ancient times the things that are not yet done, saying, My counsel shall stand, and I will do all my pleasure:

We must remember that the LORD transcends time. GOD declares that He inhabits eternity, and a day to Him is as a thousand years and a thousand years to Him is but a day (Isaiah 57:15; 2Peter 3:8). If time has a beginning or was created, then there has to be someone who started or created time. In the book of Genesis, we find that GOD created time for man. And God said, Let there be lights in the firmament of the heaven to divide the day from the night; and let them be for signs, and for seasons, and for days, and years (Genesis 1:14). When planning our future, GOD stood outside of time, and He wants us to do the same. We must transcend, go beyond, or rise above our carnal ways of thinking and planning in order to see our future as He sees it. As stated earlier, GOD knows the thoughts and plans He has for us. It may not always feel like it, but there is an expected destination. The Bible declares that all the promises of GOD are in Him yea and by His Spirit, we can say so be it (2Corinthians 1:20).

By looking at some of the synonyms for transcend, you may view the word transcend in a competitive sense. For example: outdo your competition or surpass the previous record holder (i.e., Christian McCaffrey surpassed Barry Sanders for the NCAA single-season all-purpose yards record.). However, to GOD the word transcend is not about competition or anyone else, but you. You are transcending your carnal nature and human limitations. In its root "scend" means to climb. In Genesis the twenty-eighth chapter verse twelve, Jacob stated that in his dream, he saw a ladder on earth and the top reached to heaven; and angels were ascending and descending, meaning climbing up and down the ladder. Furthermore, in the first chapter of the gospel of John verse fifty-one, Jesus stated to his disciples that they would see heaven open, and the angels of GOD ascending and descending upon him. The prefix "trans" means across or through. The prefix "trans" is used to denote movement or conveyance from one place to another or a comprehensive change. This is important to understand because for us, ascending into the spirit realm or becoming more spiritual is not enough; we must transcend our carnal ways in the process. We all will have to stand before GOD; the question is, will we be changed into the image of Christ before we stand in front of Him. In the process of climbing, there must be a movement from our ways to GOD's ways and a complete change from this world's way of thinking to GOD's way of thinking. GOD is not concerned about us outdoing or transcending each other, but He is rather concerned about us transcending above our human or sinful nature, and the limitations acquired from living in the flesh. The spirit is indeed eager and ready, but the flesh is weak (Matthew 26:41).

Romans 12:1-2 (KJV)
I beseech you therefore, brethren, by the mercies of God, that ye present your bodies a living sacrifice, holy, acceptable unto God, which is your reasonable service. Vs2 And be not conformed to this world: but be ye transformed by the renewing of your mind, that ye may prove what is that good, and acceptable, and perfect, will of God.

As we start to understand the Scriptures, we will see that becoming truly transcendent begins with changing the way we think. Romans chapter twelve verse two in the New Living Translation (NLT) says it this way, "Don't copy the behavior and customs of this world, but let God transform you into a new person by changing the way you think. Then you will learn to know God's will for you, which is good and pleasing and perfect." I have heard it said so many times that you can take a person out of the ghetto, but you can't take the ghetto out of the person. Have you ever heard that poverty is a mindset and not a state of being? You can give a person with a poverty mindset a million dollars, and they will still live in poverty because money does not change the way you think. If you think the same, you will make the same decisions. If you keep making identical decisions as you did before you had money, you will end up in the same place, and that is without money. There is a saying "A fool and his money are soon parted." It is foolishness to waste your money or allow yourself to be cheated out of it. The Scriptures go on to say, What use is it for a fool to have enough money in his hand to buy skillful and godly wisdom when he has no understanding nor does he have a desire for it (Proverbs 17:16)? This is why our thinking must become transcendent. It is not enough to increase the amount of money that we have or change how much we think about money. It is more important that we change how we view our finances, and its purpose in our lives. We must transcend our ordinary ways of thinking. A million dollars does not make us prosperous; it means that we are not broke. However, if I learn how to put a million dollars to work for me so that while I am sleeping, it is grinding and toiling on my behalf, that is the path to being financially wealthy.

In the third epistle of John, he states that above all things, he desires that we would prosper and be in health as our souls prosper. Again, the word soul in that passage of scripture is the Greek word "psuche". As stated earlier, it corresponds to our English word "psyche" which is by one definition the soul, mind, or personality of a person or group. The word "prosper" in that same passage of scripture (3John1:2) is the Greek word "euodoo" and it means to cause to prosper or be successful, to help on the road, succeed in reaching, and to grant a prosperous and expeditious journey (to lead by a direct and easy way). With this information in mind let us look at third

John chapter one verse two again. We should think of it like this. "Beloved more than anything else; I desire that your passage to success be quick and efficient, filled with help and favor that results in your prosperity in the same proportion to and at the same time as your psyche is flourishing and thriving, and receiving support while on the road to your mental growth and success." If we change the way we think; we will change the way we live. As a man thinks in his heart (nephesh, soul, mind, and psyche) so is he. Men do not judge us based on who we are on the inside. We are defined based on our outward actions. Our daily actions and behaviors are a direct extension of our current state of mind.

When it comes to making decisions, have you ever felt like there was a war going on the inside of you? If you have, you are right. That is because our flesh (carnal thoughts and desires) is antagonistic to the law of GOD. Our carnal mind does not want to submit itself to the Word of GOD nor does it not know how (Romans 8:7). The Apostle Paul stated that he had the desire to do what is moral and just; however, in his carnal mind, he did not have the power to perform that which is right in the eyes of GOD (Romans 7:18). That is why we must become more committed to our spiritual growth. This is the only way to overcome our carnal mind and pull down strongholds (attitudes and mindsets contrary to GOD) and our carnal ways of reasoning and thinking that attempt to exalt themselves above GOD and His Word. As mentioned earlier, our greatest fight with Satan is not in our body, but rather it is in our mind. The devil will use any trick as well as anyone he can to hinder us and cause to us to fall short of GOD's plan for our lives. As aforementioned, Satan will use our life experiences, disappointments, frustrations and such like in order to negatively affect our emotions pushing us down the wrong path (leading us astray). Deleterious emotions will result in undesirable behaviors. By transcending or growing in the Word of GOD we can eliminate, tear down, and lay aside every burden and sin that can so easily prevent us from running and accomplishing our goals in Christ.

If we are too emotionally burdened to the point where we feel like we cannot run, then we cannot expect to win. The race is not given to the swift nor the battle to the strong, but it is given to those that endure to the end. If we do not transcend our mere human existence that is filled with ungodly passions and desires, we may feel as if we cannot start our journey in GOD. Also, if we manage to start, we are constantly looking for an excuse to quit. Our carnal or fleshly ways will try to raise up or exalt themselves over what we have learned about our LORD and His Christ. We must continue to use the Word of GOD to cast down, demolish and utterly destroy our old mindsets and imaginations. Like a serpent, our carnal mind will try to rise up or ascend by using our fears, frustrations, and disappointments.

I have learned that when a snake has prey in its sight, it lies in wait making sure to be very still and silent. Serpents use the art of stealth to attack unsuspecting prey. However, when a snake rises up or makes noise it is trying to intimidate because it feels threatened. This is what happens with our carnal mind. As we begin to grow in GOD's word and begin to be transformed our fleshly self as well as the devil feels threatened and tries to rise up through our emotions, fears, frustrations, lusts, pride, and even our family. Remember he is not rising up because you are the prey, but because you have power and that threatens him. This is why we must continue to transcend and not just ascend. If we are ascending up a ladder, but we are still in the natural, it is easy for someone or something below us to reach up (rise up) and pull us down. However, if we transcend we are not only climbing, but we are changing and moving from a carnal to a spiritual mindset.

Isaiah 55: 7-9 (KJV)
Let the wicked forsake his way, and the unrighteous man his thoughts: and let him return unto the LORD, and he will have mercy upon him; and to our God, for he will abundantly pardon. Vs8 For my thoughts are not your thoughts, neither are your ways my ways, saith the LORD. Vs9 For as the heavens are higher than the earth, so are my ways higher than your ways, and my thoughts than your thoughts.

In the passage above we see that GOD is reminding us that His thoughts and His ways are transcendent (higher, superior, completely outside and different) compared to our thoughts and our ways. One of our biggest problems is that we bring GOD's thoughts and ways to our level instead of allowing our faith in His Word to raise our thoughts and ways to His level. Based on how we think or what we feel; we assume what GOD would say, think, or do. The prophet Isaiah is admonishing us to forsake our ways and our thoughts. In Psalm nineteen verses thirteen and fourteen, King David prayed and asked the LORD to keep him from presumptuous (arrogant, disrespectful, audacious) and willful sins. King David understands that many times we take conscious action without consulting with GOD (see Joshua 9:1-20). We are consistently warned not to think of ourselves more highly than we ought to think. However, it is in our carnal nature to think that we are right and to make decisions based on our fleshly thoughts and ways (what we think and how we feel). That is why we must transcend, discarding our natural ways and thoughts becoming more and more Christ-like as we ascend in our relationship with our Heavenly FATHER.

Romans 12:3 (KJV)
For I say, through the grace given unto me, to every man that is among you, not to think of himself more highly than he ought to think; but to think soberly, according as God hath dealt to every man the measure of faith.

Gal 6:3 KJV
For if a man think himself to be something, when he is nothing, he deceiveth himself.

THE ILLUSION OF CHOICE

Psalms 25:12 (KJV)
What man is he that feareth the LORD? Him shall he teach in the way that he shall choose

At the very beginning, a choice was placed before man; life or death, blessing, and cursing. The LORD commanded Adam not to eat of the tree of the knowledge of good and evil. The tree was in the midst of the garden, and GOD never hid it from Adam. We do not know how long Adam and Woman were in the garden before she was deceived, and Adam sinned. But we can infer that in the beginning, Adam's desire to obey GOD was greater than his will to eat from the tree; because at the start, he did not consider eating from the tree. However, Satan deceived woman giving her the illusion of choice, as a result of this deception she did eat from the tree, and now Adam is faced with another choice. However, this time Adam's will to please GOD had shifted and his will to please his wife took priority. Thus, Adam made the decision to eat, and now the rest is history (Genesis 2 and Genesis 3). Choices are easy, but decisions are hard. Adam was faced with a choice, and he then had to make a decision.

Some say that choice is an illusion created by those in power and is given to the weak. The word "illusion" is defined as something that deceives or misleads us intellectually. An illusion is also defined as the perception of something in such a way as to cause misinterpretation of its actual nature. Furthermore, an illusion is a thing that is likely to be wrongly perceived or interpreted by the senses. In other words, those in power realize that there is just one real answer; however, those without power are left with the illusion called choice. Is there really a choice when there is only one true answer? For example, if you are taking a multiple-choice exam with several different options but there is only one right/true answer. Do you really have a choice when every selection is incorrect and leads to failure except the one correct response? Failure is not a choice; it is the result of choosing the wrong answer. I have heard it said failure is not an option. No one in their right mind chooses to fail in life; the only true choice is to succeed; however, bad decisions may result in a life of failure. Thus giving the illusion that in life, we either choose to succeed or to fail. We must remember that failure was never an option. We may choose what we eat, or who we marry, or the type of car we drive, but in life, all we really want is to succeed. Therefore, we must look at our lives as a series of important decisions. Some may say that I am just arguing semantics and there is no real difference between choices and decisions. However, if we look closely, we will see that differences can be life-changing.

The word "decision" originates from a word that means cutting off. Decisions deal more with the process of organizing and analyzing information for the sole purpose of eliminating (or cutting off) all other options except the best selection. Simply put making a decision is the act of making up one's mind.   While the origin of the word "choice" means to perceive. Choice is more of a mindset. Choice is defined as an act of making a selection when faced with two or more possibilities. To have a choice means to have the right, the power, or the opportunity to choose without fear of the results or outcome. When we understand these subtle differences, we can begin to see that often times what we thought was a true choice was only an illusion.   There was a consequence associated with what we chose. Have you ever said, "If I had known this I would not have done that?" If I knew that he/she was crazy, I would not have married them. To choose means to have the ability to freely select someone or something as being the optimal or most appropriate of two or more alternatives.   How can we really choose if we have not evaluated all the options (made a decision)? Please understand that in order to make a decision we must have multiple options, and true decisions can only happen when we are able to analyze all viable options and cut them off one by one until we arrive at the best option.

Choice in its purest sense is having the ability to make a selection without analyzing and evaluating all viable options. Therefore, to have a true choice, we must be in a place of freedom and liberty. If we do not have freedom or the right to choose, do we really have a choice? Some people do not care about the result, as long as they are given the opportunity to make a selection. Some people will continue to work and be treated like slaves, as long as they feel as if they have a choice to work or not. Have you ever heard someone say, if they keep treating me like this, I am going to quit? Question, is quitting a viable possibility? Do you know anyone that got so mad on the job that they quit without weighing their options? If they did not analyze all the feasible options did they really make a decision or did they react based on their feeling? Did their emotions take them over? Have you ever been out to eat with some friends and there is always one person that looks like they are analyzing every item on the menu? They are trying to find all the worthwhile options and then make a decision on what to order. What about the person that cannot seem to make up their mind? It looks like they are in anguish. They look and look, and then finally they choose something. Did they decide or did they give the illusion of choice? More often than not, they reacted emotionally choosing something just to get it over with. You see their choice was merely an illusion. They did not make a conscious decision. They had a knee-jerk reaction. What happens when their food arrives? In many instances, they did not want what they ordered. This is because they did not make a conscious decision. Question, would that person feel pressured if they could try everything on the menu free of charge? Would they change their mind after they have tasted everything and then made a decision on what they wanted? Well-thought-out and informed decisions usually do not change but ill-advised, haphazard, hasty, abrupt, or impetuous choices are oftentimes subject to change. When we decide to take action on something, it should be settled in our hearts.

Decisions are driven more by needs, goals, and problems than by simply encountering a set of options. Our value system influences our decisions and ultimately the choices that we make. If we cannot see the innate worth of a thing, or if we do not want nor do we appreciate it; we will consequently cut it off. In the natural, we would choose something because of what it has to offer or based on how much we cherished it. Choice then is the selection from remaining treasured alternatives. I ask you again what if there are no other alternatives do you really have a choice. In that situation, you either act, or you do not. You see that is not about choice but rather motivation and desire. As stated before, several people said they have made the choice of Christ; however, they do not have the inner drive to follow him.

Who is Jesus? Select all that apply. (You must select all of the correct responses to receive credit)
a. A fraud
b. The way
c. John the Baptist's cousin
d. The Word of GOD made flesh
e. The atoning sacrifice for our sins
f. Just another dude trying to get over
g. Our Redeemer
h. The Son of GOD

In the question above there appears to be multiple correct choices (responses) available; however, each response individually is only a part of the combination. Three right and one wrong answer would leave the safe locked. We can only open the lock when we know the entire combination. There are multiple numbers but just one accurate combination; hence, there is only one complete and true choice. Letters B and D are correct; however, in light of all the other choices to say that Jesus is the way and the Word of GOD made flesh alone, would not tell us completely who he is. Thus, letters B and D only gave us the illusion of choice but choosing those selections merely would lead to failure, and failure is not an option. Only after being able to effectively and accurately organize and analyze the options can we choose (make a decision).

This is funny but often times; men think that they chose their wife when in all actuality, he did not choose his wife without her first choosing him. The Bible declares that a man that finds a wife finds a good thing and obtains favor from the LORD (Proverbs 18:22). The man approaches her, but he is not in the position to choose because he is not in control or in the place of power. Remember, he asks her and she has the right or the power to say yes or no without fear of the outcome. So his approaching her creates an illusion that he is choosing her. I have heard it said that a woman knows and chooses the man she wants to marry then puts herself in a submissive position to be chosen. So when the guy approaches her, he does not understand that he did not choose her, he had already been chosen by her. If she had not chosen him, he would never be able to approach her without being rejected. Remember true choice says I have the option to choose whatever I want without fear of failure or rejection. Animals instinctively understand this process of choosing. As with several animal species, the males fight for the right to mate with the females. Only when the male is victorious does he have the right to select any female without fear of rejection. Some eagles when the males desire to mate with a female, he must seemingly pass a series of flying tests. Now tell me, if you have to fight, pass a test or audition for the part, are you in control and are you the one choosing?

Are you the one that is analyzing viable options with the intent to make a decision? If we think about it; the males are auditioning for the part. The word "audition" means to test or to try out. It is a trial performance that gives us the opportunity to appraise or evaluate the merits of someone or something. Football players go through a series of tryouts, hoping that a professional team will choose them in the draft. When we are able to demonstrate that we are a necessary asset, or after we have proven our value, only then will one or more teams consider extending an offer. You can only play for one team at a time; therefore, you only need one offer. Question, is that having a choice? If your goal was to play in the NFL, all you need is one team to extend a contract offer to you. If that is the case, you have reached your goal, but you do not have any choice as to what team because there is only one. It is difficult to negotiate a contract when the team has multiple options of players to choose from; however, you do not have options of teams. What if we flip the script? You are considered such a high valued asset, and now multiple teams would like to offer you. Are you now in the position to choose? Not only are you able to select from the possible options of teams, but you are also capable of negotiating a better contract. That is the power of true choice. That is the power of the blessing. However, we must remember that in many instances we cannot choose until you have first been chosen. Heaven or hell is a no brainer, nevertheless, we cannot choose heaven unless I have been chosen by GOD first. Hence, Jesus said no man can come unto him except the FATHER first draws them (John 6:44 and John 6:65).

Ephesians 1:4
According as he hath chosen us in him before the foundation of the world that we should be holy and without blame before him in love.

As Christians, we sometimes have the illusion that we have chosen Christ. When it is He that has chosen us. Jesus told his disciples "you have not chosen me, but I have chosen you" (Matthew 22:14; John 15:16-19). Some might argue and say that we had to choose Christ also; however, it is more like we accepted his offer. Can we negotiate the terms of the contract? Is there another offer on the table that is just as desirable if not more desirable as Christ's offer? The Bible says that many are called, but few are chosen. I have been taught to understand that as believers in Jesus Christ, we have to choose to be chosen, in other words, we accept or deny his plan of salvation. Our calling upon GOD gives us the illusion that we chose Him, and we are in control. However, we are not in control of GOD nor are we in a position of power over Him. John the Baptist told the Pharisees and Sadducees that GOD could wipe them out and use stones to raise up children unto Abraham (Matthew 3:9). The LORD has options, and He can make a choice without fear of the outcome. GOD is so powerful that He empowers us with gifts, and He is not afraid if we use them for other purposes than His. Question, did you review all the information and made a conscious decision to accept GOD's offer of salvation or did you make a hasty choice based on your emotions? Is Satan's or any other being's offer as good as what the LORD has offered? I assure you that no one or nothing can compare to GOD and what Christ has done. My prayer is that we all continue to grow in the Word of GOD and make a clear and conscious decision to accept the LORD and His offer without fear but with overwhelming joy and confidence in the outcome.

1Corinthians 1:26-31 (AMPC)
For [simply] consider your own call, brethren; not many [of you were considered to be] wise according to human estimates and standards, not many influential and powerful, not many of high and noble birth. Vs27 [No] for God selected (deliberately chose) what in the world is foolish to put the wise to shame, and what the world calls weak to put the strong to shame. Vs28 And God also selected (deliberately chose) what in the world is lowborn and insignificant and branded and treated with contempt, even the things that are nothing, that He might depose and bring to nothing the things that are, Vs29 So that no mortal man should [have pretense for glorying and] boast in the presence of God. Vs30 But it is from Him that you

have your life in Christ Jesus, Whom God made our Wisdom from God, [revealed to us a knowledge of the divine plan of salvation previously hidden, manifesting itself as] our Righteousness [thus making us upright and putting us in right standing with God], and our Consecration [making us pure and holy], and our Redemption [providing our ransom from eternal penalty for sin]. Vs31 So then, as it is written, Let him who boasts and proudly rejoices and glories, boast and proudly rejoice and glory in the Lord.

Another word for choice is abundance and only in abundance is their choice. If we were to buy a car, we would look at the style of the car as well as the accessories that come with the car to help us make our decision. Some people will drive an eight-year-old car not because they want to, but because that is the only car, they can afford. It may be a Honda, Ford, etc., and you think you had a choice and chose the car you wanted. However, if you can only afford a $3,000.00 car, then you did not have a choice. You had to get an older model car because that is all that you can afford. True choice says I have enough money that I can buy any car I want, and I choose to buy a Ford or Dodge, etc. My money did not limit what I wanted, but my decision did. If you only had one suit you do not have a choice; therefore, you do not have to decide on what suit you can wear. Solely in abundance is there a true choice. Remember, Jesus declared that he is the only way, and he is the only door. So when it comes to eternal life, there is not an abundance of choices, there is only CHRIST JESUS. Any other answer is wrong, and it will result in failure. Remember, failure is not an option.

Some believe that we have already made a choice, and this life is the process of figuring out why we have made that choice. With this in mind, it is difficult to see beyond the choices that we do not understand, in other words, ignorance leads to indecision. We spend our lifetime trying to figure out "why" and accomplish our purpose for being on this earth. The decisions we make are based on fulfilling our purpose and achieving destiny. However, we cannot decide if we do not know our "what," let alone our "why." Only when we are fulfilling our purpose, do we sincerely experience a sense of success or accomplishment. Some say we were created simply to love and worship GOD. If this alone was true, why is it that most Christians who experience a life-changing encounter with GOD become unsatisfied with their lives as usual? They begin to sense and enquire about a greater purpose for their lives. A father does not base his success on how many children he has, but on the outcome of his children. However, to improve the outcome of his children, a father must first understand his function, responsibility, and purpose. The child's upbringing and not the maturity of the child becomes the gage used to determine the successful completion of the father's purpose. The child may become a menace to society; at the same time, this does not mean that the father did not function according to his purpose or fulfill his responsibility.

Romans chapter eight verse twenty-six says for we know that all things work together for the good of them that love the LORD and are the called according to his purpose. Remember GOD knows the end and middle from the beginning. This is important to understand because it is our responsibility to decide to function in our purpose, and it is His responsibility to make our purpose clear as well make it all work together for our good. Our willingness to serve the LORD cannot be a function of mere choice as if there are multiple competing offers; but rather, we must make a conscious decision to serve Him as if no other option exists. Going back to Egypt is not an option. Staying in the wilderness will not do. I have decided to follow Jesus, and there is no turning back.

CONCLUSION

This book was not designed to provide the answers, but rather to provoke deep thought and inward reflection as we travel down the path of self-discovery. It was written to cause us to investigate our thoughts and actions learning to distinguish between GOD's truth, and that which we have allowed ourselves to accept as truth. Having the ability to know GOD's truth gives us a fighting chance to contest opinions, philosophies, thoughts, and every proud and vain imagination that tries to exalt itself above the true knowledge of GOD. We now understand that; although we live in the flesh our warfare is not carnal, and as a result, we should not be fighting in our flesh or with natural weapons. Our true weapons are from GOD, and they give us the power to destroy mindsets, attitudes, and false perceptions.

Hopefully, we have a better understanding of the role that our body was supposed to play versus the role it plays in our everyday carnal nature. We started this journey looking at outward factors and began to explore our soul more intimately. The prophet Nathan did the same thing with King David. He did not merely go to the King and say look at what you did. No, he started with a story concerning a man taking another person's lamb. This allowed David to see his wrong from a distance. Most of us can see everyone else's wrong, but we have a hard time seeing our own. Everyman's behavior and actions are right in their own eyes. The Prophet started King David's journey with his eyes and his finger pointing outward condemning the man for his actions (taking the lamb). Afterward, Nathan turned the King's focus inward causing him to see that he had done the very same thing. As a result, David was able to acknowledge that he had sinned against the LORD (2Samuel 1:14). Many theologians believe it is because of this situation that David wrote psalms fifty-one.

My desire is that as we take this journey, we learn to use the Word of GOD to change the way we act and think. We must understand that the LORD never told us that everything would be easy; therefore, we should not always be looking for the easy way out. The Word of GOD declares that He would keep us in perfect peace if we stayed focused on Him. Remember, the LORD wants us to see as He sees. It is essential that we learn to zoom in as well as focus on GOD, allowing us to see the fine details of His masterpiece being revealed in our everyday lives. So many times, we miss the forest because of the trees. Scientists have identified that our bodies are made up of trillions of cells that are so finely detailed, working together to perform common functions such as breathing, seeing and hearing. Our ability to think and create is a true miracle in its own right. We understand that powerful computers and machines with artificial intelligence have been created by man and yet many people choose to believe that our very existence is by happenstance. They have made a choice not to believe in our Creator because they refuse to evaluate what GOD has given as a sign.

Many individuals use arguments from ignorance (appeal to ignorance) in an attempt to make their unsubstantiated claims appear to be true. They simply believe what they are saying is true because no one has physically proven that what they believe is false. In other words, many have attempted to shift the burden of proof on the believer. The atheist says that GOD does not exist because in their mind there is not enough information to disprove their belief. A scientist can say that there was a big bang, causing all life to randomly occur and accept that as true because none of us were physically there to provide arguments that refute their statement. They have placed the burden of truth on the believer. You see the non-believer want us to make the unseen GOD visible without using the natural things that the LORD has given us to prove His existence. The Bible declares that He has manifested His divine nature and power through the things that He has made; so all men are without excuse if they choose not to believe or acknowledge Him (Romans 1:19-20). Hebrew eleven verse three declares by our innate trust and enduring confidence in the power, wisdom, and goodness of God (faith) we understand that time (the ages) and the worlds (the universe) were framed and created by the Word of GOD. The scriptures declare everything that we see was initially made out of what we cannot see. Proof of GOD's existence is all around us as well as in us. You see they want a clear choice, but the LORD wants all of us to make an informed decision and accept his call to salvation. If there was a beginning of time, who started the clock?

You were not created by happenstance, but you were created for a purpose. You are fearfully and wonderfully made. You are GOD's handiwork. Just because we have not identified our purpose, does not mean that we do not have a purpose. This is why we have started this journey into our soul. We are learning to move our human nature with all of its proclivities out of the way and attempting to see ourselves the way GOD wants to see us. As we begin to walk in a new level of enlightenment, we understand even more we are not there yet. Wherever there is, we realize that we have not made it to that specific place in our inner man. Remember, we are a work in progress; therefore, our journey continues.

Made in the USA
Columbia, SC
13 April 2019